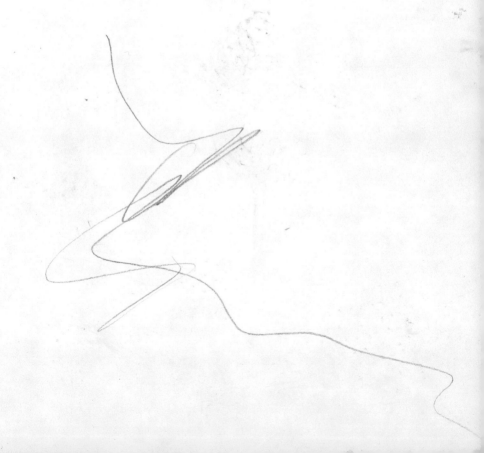

THE GOLFER'S
REPAIR AND
MAINTENANCE
HANDBOOK

THE GOLFER'S
REPAIR AND
MAINTENANCE
HANDBOOK

JOHN C. HARVEY

Contemporary Books, Inc.
Chicago

796.35
H26

Library of Congress Cataloging in Publication Data

Harvey, John C.
   The golfer's repair and maintenance handbook.

   Includes index.
   1. Golf—Equipment and supplies—Maintenance and
repair.   I. Title.
GV976.H37   1984   796.352'028   84-5802
ISBN 0-8092-5448-4

Published by Contemporary Books, Inc.
180 North Michigan Avenue, Chicago, Illinois 60601
Manufactured in the United States of America
Library of Congress Catalog Card Number: 84-5802
International Standard Book Number: 0-8092-5448-4

Published simultaneously in Canada by Beaverbooks, Ltd.
195 Allstate Parkway, Valleywood Business Park
Markham, Ontario L3R 4T8 Canada

CONTENTS

INTRODUCTION

This book is written for the 16 million men and women golfers who venture forth regularly to wear out their golf grips, beat the glossy finish off their fine woods, and bend or break a shaft now and then. It is written for the golfers who, when their clubs are worn and mutilated, wonder if those battered old sticks just might be affecting their game.

The answer, I can tell you, is "Yes!" Poorly maintained clubs *do* affect your game. You will play with more confidence and score lower if your clubs are in top shape. And so this book is intended to give you new understanding of the clubs you play with and to show you how to keep heavily-played clubs in top condition.

The average golfer is often intimidated by the thought of golf club repairs and by golf club repair talk. The skills needed to regrip a set of clubs or refinish a set of woods are generally believed to fall somewhere between computer design and advanced brain surgery.

But golf clubs are really very simple to work with, and a few easy repairs can improve your game substantially. A new set of golf grips, for instance, can help you hit straighter, farther, and with less shock to your hands; I have seen a new set of grips actually take eight or nine strokes off a golfer's game. A slightly altered hitting angle on the face of your woods or irons can help you get the ball up in the air better. A simple repair such as replacing a broken shaft can restore a full set of woods or irons to useful play. Minor adjustments can help correct a hook or slicing problem with your wood shots. And there are many more easy jobs the amateur can do and benefit from.

This book is intended to introduce golfers to an entirely new phase of the game we all enjoy so much. Now, let's tee it up and hit on down the fairway.

1
WHY LEARN TO DO GOLF REPAIRS?

Why would anyone want to do his or her own golf club repairs? I can suggest several reasons why.

- One, it's an interesting hobby and it's fun. You learn something new about golf. Everybody has read how Arnie and Tom and Jack tinker with their clubs in their own workshops. And now you're doing it, too, just like they do. What class!
- Two, you get club repairs such as regripping and refinishing done much faster when you do your own. There's no waiting while the golf shop repairman works down a long list. Or no waiting for old Joe, the local repairman, to come back from a long vacation. You do your own and they're ready right away, with no time lost.
- Three, you control the quality of repairs. Before long you'll be doing as good a job as or better than the local repairman because you take extra pains, and he has 20 golfers yelling at him to get their jobs done faster.

1

- Four, you impress your golfing buddies tremendously with comments such as, "My grips seem a little slick so I'm putting on a new set of Green Victories for the tournament this weekend." Or, "I took out two points of swing weight and, boy, am I hitting the ball better."
- And five, you save some dollars and have extra bucks for greens fees or even a short golfing vacation. Since most of the cost of golf club repairs is hand labor and overhead, material being a minor factor, doing your own can cut the cost of most repairs by three-quarters or more. Take a look at the following table and see what I mean.

Repair	Repair Shop Prices	Cost of Doing Your Own
Installing New Grips		
Rubber	$ 4.50–$ 6.00	$1.90–$2.25
Cord	$ 5.50–$ 6.75	$3.85–$4.20
Oversize	$ 5.00–$ 6.50	$2.00–$2.25
Leather	$ 9.00–$12.00	$5.50–$7.95
Irons		
Reshafting Iron and Regripping	$13.00–$14.00	$7.25–$7.50
Tightening Head	$ 5.00–$ 7.00	$ .25
Changing Swing weight and Regripping	$ 6.00–$ 8.00	$2.50
Shortening Shaft and Regripping	$ 8.00–$ 9.00	$1.90–$2.25
Lengthening Shaft and Regripping	$ 9.00–$12.00	$2.60–$3.00

Repair	Repair Shop Prices	Cost of Doing Your Own
Installing New Grips		
Woods		
Refinishing Clubhead with New Whipping	$12.00-$16.00	$2.30
Tightening Head	$ 6.50-$12.00	$ .25
Reshafting with New Grip	$14.00-$18.00	$7.80
Replacing Insert and Refinishing	$17.00-$18.00	$2.65
Changing Loft on Woods and Resealing	$12.50-$16.00	$ .15 (for spray)
New Whipping	$ 3.00-$ 4.50	$ .39

2

THE NOMENCLATURE OF WOODS AND IRONS

When working with woods and irons as a hobby, it is very helpful to have a working knowledge of the nomenclature of these clubs. Even if you already know the names of the parts of golf clubs, a review may be helpful.

WOOD CLUBS

Look at the head-on view of a wood club (Figure 2-A) and identify its parts.

2-A. Head of a wood club

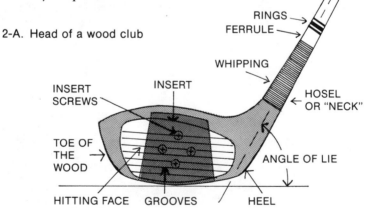

RINGS
FERRULE
WHIPPING
INSERT SCREWS
INSERT
HOSEL OR "NECK"
TOE OF THE WOOD
ANGLE OF LIE
HITTING FACE   GROOVES   HEEL

The *insert* is that plastic inlay in the center of the hitting face that runs from the sole plate to the top of the head. The insert's purpose is to take the shock and wear when the golf ball is hit. Although usually red or black, inserts may be some other color. The *insert screws* may secure the insert to the wood, although the insert is cemented in with epoxy and the screws may be purely for decoration. When you hear a pro say, "Boy, he really hit it on the screws!" then you know that he means a player hit the ball dead center.

The *hitting face* is the entire hitting area of the wood, which includes the laminated wooden (maple or persimmon) area as well as the insert. The *grooves* are those horizontal cuts made in the hitting face of the wood.

The toe of the wood is the outboard end of the wood head. It corresponds to the toes of a human foot, as the club's heel corresponds to the heel of a human foot.

The *whipping* is the black or colored winding thread wrapped tightly around the neck, or *hosel,* of a wood club. The whipping's purpose is to prevent the wood from splitting when the ball is struck. Above the whipping are the *ferrule* and *rings.* The ferrule is that black plastic sleeve on the shaft that abuts the wood. The rings, of course, are the colored rings located above the ferrule, on the shaft.

Angles of Lie and Loft

The *angle of lie* is the angle between the club's shaft and the ground when the club is in the position of address. For example, a driver may have a 54-degree angle of lie; a flat-lie driver may have only a 52-degree angle of lie; and a No. 3 wood, because it's a shorter club with a shorter shaft, may have a 55-degree angle of lie.

To see the *angle of loft* of a wood, look at it from the toe of the club toward the hosel (Figure 2-B). The angle of loft is the angle between the hitting face and a line perpendicular to the ground. Drivers usually have a 10- or 11-degree angle of loft. A hitter who has a tendency to sky the ball or hit his tee shots too high

2-B. Heads of a driver and a 3 wood

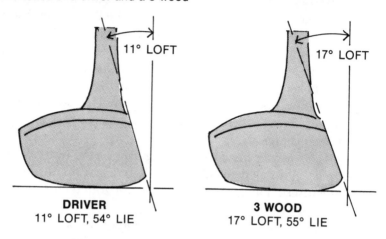

DRIVER
11° LOFT, 54° LIE

3 WOOD
17° LOFT, 55° LIE

may customize his driver's hitting face to have only a 9-degree angle of loft. Similarly, a player who has a chronic tendency to hit his tee shots too low may customize his hitting face to have a 12-degree angle of loft. As in Figure 2-B, a 3 wood commonly has a 17-degree angle of loft, although the angle may be 16 or 18 degrees, depending on the club's maker.

The angle of loft increases in increments of approximately 3 degrees per club. Thus, if the 3 wood's angle of loft were 17 degrees, that of the 5 wood would be about 23 degrees, and so on. The angle of lie, however, increases much more slowly than the angle of loft; from a driver to a 3 wood, the angle of lie increases only about 1 degree, while the angle of loft increases about 6 degrees.

THE SOLE

Figure 2-C is a view of the *sole* of a wood, as the entire area that rests on the ground is called. The *sole plate* is the stamped metal plate that prevents wear to the bottom of the club. *Sole plate screws* hold the sole plate in position. The name of the club, stamped into the metal, is referred to as the *stamping*, and the color is the *paint fill*. The small hole with an allen screw in some wood heads is a *swing weighting port,* which is where lead powder or lead shot can be added to increase the swing weight or removed to decrease the swing weight of the club.

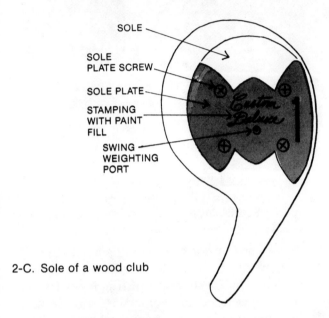

SOLE

SOLE
PLATE SCREW

SOLE PLATE

STAMPING
WITH PAINT
FILL

SWING
WEIGHTING
PORT

2-C. Sole of a wood club

TYPES OF WOOD FACES

The differences among a square face, a slice face, and a hook face of a wood club are apparent in Figure 2-D.

A *square face* is one with zero degrees of built-in hook or slice. Theoretically, with a perfect swing, a wood with a square face would drive the ball straight down the fairway. Most manufactured golf woods are made with a square face, although some manufacturers give the woods about 1 degree of hook to compensate for the average golfer's tendency to slice the ball.

An *open* or *slice face* is suitable for a golfer who has a strong tendency to hook the ball. Notice that as the club comes through at the point of impact, the angle of the hitting face is centered slightly off to the right. This might be a 2- or 3-degree slice. When the hitting face comes across the ball at an angle, it tends to give the ball a clockwise spin, which results in a slice.

2-D. Heads of wood clubs

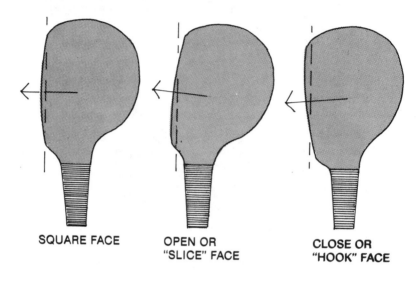

SQUARE FACE   OPEN OR   CLOSE OR
                        "SLICE" FACE   "HOOK" FACE

A wood head with a *closed* or *hook face* (exaggeratedly represented in Figure 2-D) would be good for a golfer who has a strong tendency to slice the ball. When this hitting face strikes a ball squarely, it tends to give it a counterclockwise spin, so that the ball spins in the same direction as a curve ball thrown by a right-handed baseball pitcher. As a result, the ball tends to hook off to the left as it goes down the fairway.

BULGE AND ROLL

Normally, the hitting face of a well-made, factory-manufactured wood club is not absolutely flat; there is a slight, two-way curve in the face. The curve in the hitting face from side to side is referred to as the *bulge,* and the curve in the hitting face from top to bottom is referred to as the *roll.* (See Figure 2-E.) Bulge and roll are built into a wood so that its hitting face will touch the golf ball at only one point instead of on a broad surface. The radius of the bulge and roll may be 9, 10, or 12 inches. A 10-inch radius is probably most common for factory-manufactured clubs.

2-E. Heads of wood clubs

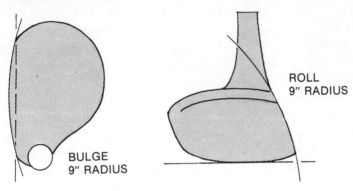

BULGE
9" RADIUS

ROLL
9" RADIUS

If necessary, the bulge and roll can be altered, with the aid of a simple *bulge and roll gauge,* a metal template that is held against the wood face either from side to side or vertically to check the bulge and roll. With a flat file, it is possible to remove wood from the top and bottom and more wood from the right and left sides to convert a 10-inch radius into an 8-inch radius. On the other hand, by removing a slight amount of wood from the center, at the high point of the bulge and the high point of the roll, you can convert a 10-inch radius into a 12-inch radius.

IRON CLUBS

Look at Figure 2-F, a head-on view of the head of an iron club, to review the nomenclature of irons.

2-F. Head of an iron club

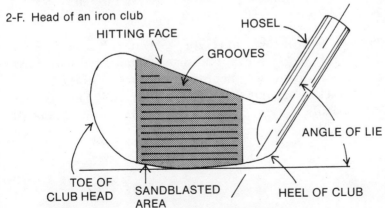

HITTING FACE

HOSEL

GROOVES

ANGLE OF LIE

TOE OF
CLUB HEAD

SANDBLASTED
AREA

HEEL OF CLUB

The *hitting face* extends from the *toe* of the club to its *heel*. The *sandblasted area* is the center portion of the club with a sandblasted roughness in the middle, which puts bite and spin on the ball when it is hit. The *grooves* also help put spin on a ball hit with an iron. The iron's *angle of lie* corresponds with the angle of lie of a wood club.

An iron club's *angle of loft* is the angle between the shaft and the hitting face. Figure 2-G shows a 2 iron with a 21-degree angle of loft and a 58-degree angle of lie and a 7 iron with a 38-degree angle of loft and a 62-degree angle of lie. These angles are fairly representative but, as with woods, irons' angles of loft may vary a degree or two in either direction, depending on the manufacturer.

2-G. Heads of iron clubs

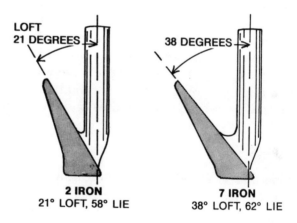

The other side of the iron (Figure 2-H) reveals a *cavity-back head*, currently very popular. The metal of an iron with a cavity-back head is thinnest right behind the sweet spot of the hitting area and thickest around the outside of the club. The *hosel* or neck, the *ferrule*, the *rings*, and the *shaft* of the iron club are all shown as well.

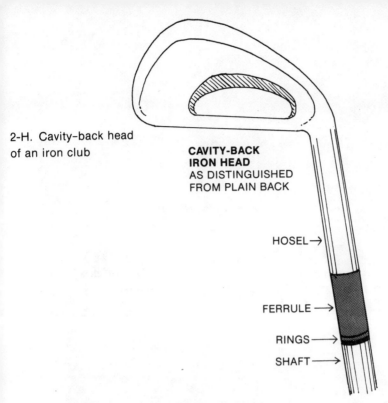

2-H. Cavity–back head of an iron club

CAVITY-BACK IRON HEAD
AS DISTINGUISHED FROM PLAIN BACK

HOSEL →

FERRULE →

RINGS →

SHAFT →

GRIPS FOR WOODS AND IRONS

The grips of both wood and iron clubs have the same nomenclature. (See Figure 2-I.) The top, or the big end, of the grip is known as the *end cap*. The design or *pattern* of the grip is molded into the rubber or stamped into the leather, and the color pattern is known as the *paint fill*. Moving down the grip toward the head, you can see that the grip is trimmed by a *grip collar* at the point where the *shaft* enters the grip.

The various types of grips available and how to regrip clubs yourself are discussed in Chapter 4.

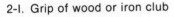

2-I. Grip of wood or iron club

END CAP OF GRIP ↓

PAINT FILL IN GRIP PATTERN ↓

GRIP COLLAR ↓   SHAFT ↓

3
TOOLS REQUIRED FOR GOLF CLUB REPAIRS

Before taking up the various repair jobs that a golfer can do at home, we should look at the small tools most commonly used when repairing golf clubs. Small repair jobs go much more quickly and easily if just the right small tool is available. Take a look at many of the simple tools found in a small golf repair workshop and see what they do for you.

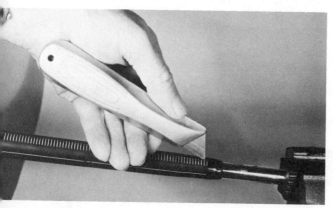

3-1. **Utility Knife.** A metal utility knife belongs in every workshop. Use it to slit and remove old grips, clean out grooves, cross threads, cross slots in insert screws and sole plate screws, and in many other instances when a sharp edge is helpful.

3-2. **Golf Shaft Gauge.** One side of this simple gauge measures the butt size or the large end of golf club shafts, so that you know which grip or shaft extender to order. The other side measures grip sizes, so that you can tell whether a grip is oversize, regular, or perhaps ladies' size.

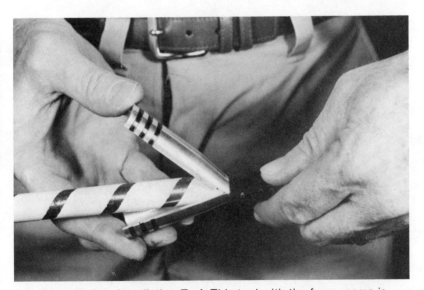

3-3. **Duckbill Grip Installation Tool.** This tool with the funny name is used when you are installing a new set of grips. The tool comes in two pieces. You fit one on each side of the shaft and press them together, which stretches the open end of the grip so that it can get started over the tape and over the shaft.

3-4. **Groove Cleaner.** A groove cleaner has a 90-degree carbide tip that is used to clean out the grooves on iron clubs.

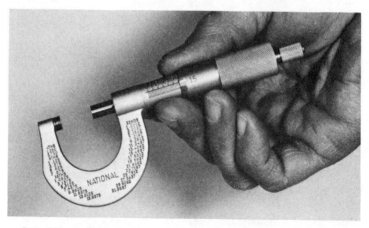

3-5. **Micrometer.** A micrometer is handy to have in a golf repair workshop. You can use it to measure the butt and tip sizes of shafts exactly, so that you're sure what part size is called for.

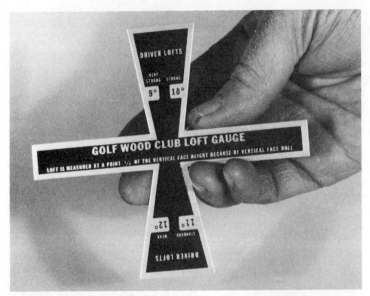

3-6. **Driver Loft Gauge.** A driver loft gauge measures the angle of loft on the hitting face of your No. 1 wood. Common lofts for drivers are 9 degrees, 10 degrees, and 11 degrees, and this gauge measures them and tells you your club's loft angle.

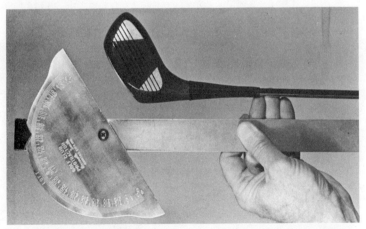

3-7. **Loft and Lie Protractor.** This device is used to measure the loft and lie of both woods and irons. It gives you a reading in degrees, and it is simple to use and understand.

3-8. **Vise Pads.** These tools are thick felt pads cemented to a section of plywood that straddles a center shaft of a workbench vise. Use them on each side of a wood head when you lock a head in the vise to work on the sole plate or the face insert.

3-9. **Radius Gauge.** A radius gauge gives you bulge and roll readings on the hitting face of a wood. The face of a good wood is not absolutely flat; it has a slightly convex curve to it, and this gauge tells you whether the curve is 8, 9, 10, or 12 degrees.

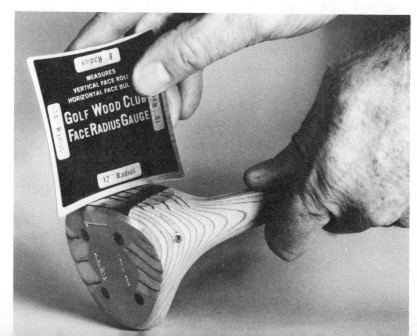

3-10. Vise Clamp. A vise clamp is a rubber block, slit lengthwise, that snaps around the shaft of a golf club. It is then clamped between the jaws of a vise to protect the shaft from being scratched or crushed. It is very handy for installing new grips, and you receive a free new vise clamp when you order 14 or more new grips.

3-11. Golf Shaft Tip Gauge. This gauge measures the tip or small end of a golf shaft that fits into the club head. It's very important to know the exact tip size of the shaft before ordering a new one. This gauge will tell you the size with an accuracy of 2- or 3-thousandths of an inch.

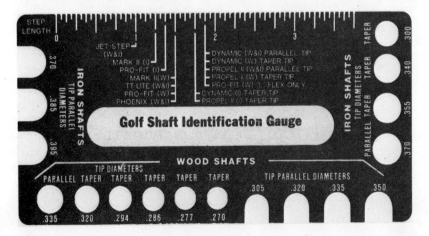

4
GRIPS
TYPES OF GRIPS AND REGRIPPING YOUR CLUBS

How is your golf game, anyway? Are the clubs slipping and turning in your hands? Are you pushing a lot of shots off to the right? Topping a lot of balls down the fairway? If so, you'd better take a good look at the type and condition of the grips on your clubs.

Grips are the "handles" on your clubs that provide the important link between you, the golfer, and the club that hits the ball. The many types of grips available today—grips made of rubber, leather, and cord, oversized grips, and grips made especially for the golfers with extra-large or arthritic hands—are discussed in this chapter.

But no matter what type the grip is, if it is old and slick, it will cause a lot of problems. New golf grips have a clinging quality or "tacky" feel. They cling to your hands during the swing; they won't slip and turn. So you really do hit better, straighter, and longer down the fairway and save strokes. When grips get slick and worn, losing their tackiness, they are apt to twist and slip in your hands, so that you hit a lot of bad balls that you wish you could call back.

The pros know how important saving just one or two strokes can be, and they know how important new grips can be. These athletes may hit 1,200 to 1,500 balls a week—as many as some golfers hit in a whole season. Therefore, after three or four weeks of regular practice and play, pros' golf grips become a little worn and lose that nice tacky cling and soft feel. Thus, most touring pros put on a new set of golf grips every four or five weeks. One top money winner who is especially fussy about his equipment may change grips as often as every week or 10 days.

So what does this mean to you? Why, it means that you really will play better golf with new grips on your clubs every season—or maybe twice a season, if you play three or four times a week. Your first time out with new grips, you will swear you are hitting with new clubs. You will hit better and your score should come down a few strokes.

Regripping your clubs yourself is very economical. As for how much money you will save by doing your own regripping, let's see: Your friendly neighborhood pro shop probably charges $5.00, or $5.50, or even $6.00 a grip. And 14 clubs at $6.00 a grip comes to $84.00. However, you can order a set of new grips by mail for about $2.00 a grip, put them on yourself, and save $40, maybe even $50.

4-1. Check grips often for signs of wear. These grips need to be replaced. Notice that the pattern is partly worn away and that the surface is hard and brittle.

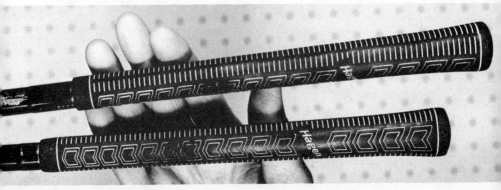

TYPES OF GRIPS

The type of grip you use on your clubs has a significant effect on your golf game. Pro golfers, when not hitting well, may switch grips in an attempt to find a type that allows them to hit better and thus improve their games. The variety of grips available and the advantages and disadvantages of each type are described in this section.

RUBBER GRIPS

Rubber grips are the most economical type of grip, as they tend to last the longest. All rubber grips are slip-on grips, and they are considered to be standard. The most obvious advantage of these grips is their "tacky" feel that most golfers prefer.

LEATHER GRIPS

Leather grips come in two varieties, slip-on and wrap-on.

Slip-On Leather Grips

Slip-on leather grips, the most traditional grips, have the tacky quality of rubber, but they are two to three times more expensive than rubber grips. Many golfers choose these because they are soft to the touch.

Wrap-On Leather Grips

Wrap-on leather grips seem to be favored by low-handicap golfers, who also tend to be the long, powerful hitters. A high percentage of touring pros are known to use wrap-on leather grips regularly.

Golfers go to the wrap-on leather grips in the belief that these grips have less torque, or twisting and turning effect, as the golfer comes into the hit and through his or her swing. This claim that these grips have less torque is based on the fact that, if you turn a rubber grip on a shafted club in your hand, you can feel the rubber give slightly in either direction as you apply pressure. When you turn a wrap-on grip in your hand, it has less give or stretch than the rubber has. Leather wrap-on grips are only made by Lamkin and Neumann.

CORD GRIPS

Somewhere along the line, you may have run into some funny-looking grips called *cord grips*, which actually have auto tire cord embedded in the rubber compound to provide a better grip and traction.

There are several advantages to cord grips. The main advantage is that the cord tread gives you a very secure grip, even under bad weather conditions. Cord grips are less likely to slip in your hands when you are playing in the rain. These grips are also very good in a hot, moist climate. If you often play under hot, humid conditions in which your hands perspire a lot, you will find cord grips helpful.

Look at the cord grips shown in Photo 4-2. At the top is a Crown cord grip, which has the same design as the very popular Men's Crown grip, except for the bits of cord embedded in the rubber compound. The Crown cord grip gives you super gripping power and traction and is one of the all-time favorite designs.

The second grip from the top is the Victory velvet cord grip, which has the favorite Green Victory design on the black rubber

4-2. Five types of cord grips, from top to bottom: the Crown cord grip, the Victory velvet cord grip, the All Velvet cord grip, the Classic cord grip, and the Cord Line cord grip.

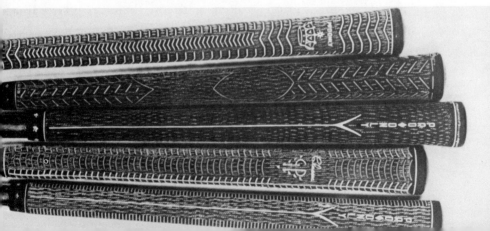

compound. This grip, while still a very tough, all-weather blend, has less cord in it, making it easier on the hands.

In the center is the All Velvet cord grip. This grip sells well because it's so easy on your hands since it is made with only half the usual amount of cord. So it has the nice, velvety feel of rubber as well as good traction for the cord in the compound.

The fourth cord grip in this lineup is the Classic cord grip. Again, actual fabric cord is molded into this famous rubber and cork compound to guarantee no slipping and turning as the ball is hit.

At the bottom is what is called the Cord Line grip, a pro-only design with outstanding gripping power. Real cord is embedded throughout the compound of softer rubber.

There's no doubt that a cord grip is a rough, rugged grip for golfers with rough, rugged hands. The cord mixture, while providing better traction under wet and slippery conditions, does quickly wear out golf gloves and callouses hands. Cord grips are long-lasting, long-wearing, and good-hitting and are sold at a somewhat premium price. You probably won't find these grips in a regular pro shop, but they are available by mail.

OVERSIZED GRIPS

Oversized grips are becoming increasingly popular as golfers learn about and ask for them. Generally speaking, oversized grips are meant for golfers with big hands. If you stand 6'4" tall with big hands to match, the ordinary grip feels as small as a pencil in your left hand when you stand up to swing. Your fingers wrap around too far and it is difficult to get a good, firm grip. For this reason, golfers with big hands tend to like oversized grips.

Golfers with arthritic hands also may find that oversized grips improve their games. A grip with a larger circumference fills out the hand better and affords stiff and sore fingers a more secure grip.

Oversized grips are made with extra-thick rubber. The standard oversized grip's diameter is about $\frac{1}{32}$ inch greater than the diameter of a normal grip. A mere ⅟₃₂ inch in diameter doesn't sound like much, but the small increase in diameter means an even greater increase in circumference, so there's a good deal more grip to wrap your fingers around.

Oversized grips are rarely found on sale to the public, except by mail. Only one of the major grip manufacturers makes an oversized grip, Tacki-Mac (on the West coast), which has an oversized herringbone design available in both brown and black rubber material.

As an alternative to mail ordering oversized grips, you can make them yourself by converting regular rubber slip-on grips to oversized grips. (See pages 24–29.) Trying to make oversized grips out of cord or leather slip-on grips is not advised because the cord material and leather do not stretch easily.

ARTHRITIC GRIPS

Arthritis in your hands can make golf very painful and/or very frustrating. In recent years, arthritic grips have been developed which enable golfers with arthritis to play the game again. Some of these grips are extra-large so that stiffened arthritic fingers can grip them securely. And some of these grips have special shapes that keep a club locked in the fingers while it is being swung at the ball.

Not only are these grips popular with golfers who have arthritic hands, but they are also widely used by golfers without arthritis who find that they can hit better and straighter if their clubs are equipped with these specially shaped grips. This is because a once-a-week golfer may not play enough to have a strong, firm grip on his club, so he may tend to loosen his left hand at the top of the swing. And when he comes down and hits the ball, there it goes, off to the right.

Four types of arthritic grips are shown in Photo 4-3. The grip at the bottom is the Lamkin Silhouette, a specially contoured grip with a distinct bulge to fit in the fingers of the left hand. With that bulge locked in your left hand, there's less opportunity for the club to slip or change position, so you're bound to hit more straight shots that go where you're aiming.

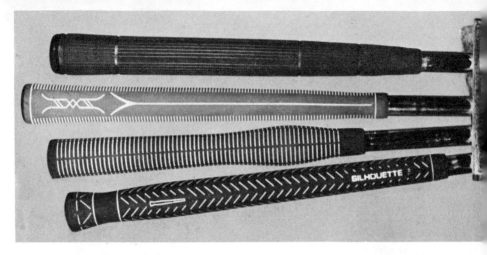

4-3. Arthritic grips are made in special shapes and sizes for golfers with arthritic hands. They have enabled many golfers to come back to the game they love. Four types of arthritic grips are shown here. From bottom to top: the Lamkin Silhouette grip, the Hour Glass grip, Eaton's arthritic grip, and the Sensation grip.

The second grip up is the Hour Glass grip, which has not one, but two distinct bulges. Again, this unique shape locks the grip, and the club, in your hands when you swing.

The third grip is Eaton's arthritic grip. It doesn't have an unusual shape but it is an oversized grip with a big, knoblike end cap that locks in your left hand if you should happen to loosen your grip just a little.

The grip on the top is the newest in the arthritic lineup, the Sensation grip by Tacki-Mac. It not only has the biggest diameter in the field (over 1 inch), but it also has an unusual crushable surface that provides a firm, nonslip grip. The Chamois grip (not shown here) by Avon is standard size but is easier on arthritic hands because it has air pockets to cushion the shock of hitting the ball.

HOW TO REGRIP YOUR CLUBS

Regripping a full set of clubs takes only a couple of hours and requires few special tools—only a vise clamp, a utility knife or single-edged razor blade, paint thinner or other solvent, double-stick tape, and a bit of epoxy. Doing your own regripping is as simple as knocking in an 8-inch putt.

INSTALLING RUBBER GRIPS

Follow these step-by-step instructions for putting on a set of new rubber grips.

On your workbench, lay out the set of grips with the strips of golf shaft tape that come with new grips so that they're handy and ready to pick up. Snap a vise clamp around the shaft of the club and then lock the square block of rubber in the vise securely. (A vise clamp is not essential, but it helps to have one on your workbench so that you can work with both hands free.)

Removing the Old Grips

To remove an old grip, with a utility knife or a single-edged razor blade, slit the old grip lengthwise all the way down to the bare metal. (See Photo 4-4.) Spread the cut edges apart and pull

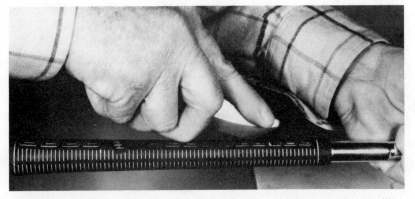

4-4. With the club locked in a vise, slit the grip lengthwise with a utility knife or even a single-edge razor blade.

the old grip off the shaft. In many cases, the layer of tape that bonds the grip to the shaft will come away with the grip, as in Photo 4-5. Sometimes, however, the pulled-away grip leaves a thin, hard layer of old tape on the shaft. When this happens, wet the old tape down with a little paint thinner or mineral spirits, using a small paintbrush. Let the solvent penetrate and soften the tape, then scrape it off with a razor blade, the blade of a screwdriver, or a utility knife.

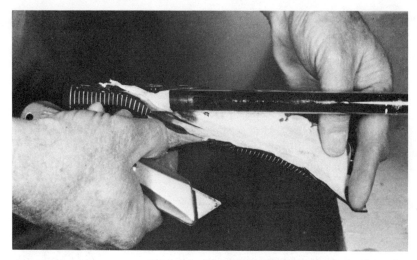

4-5. Pull the old grip off of the shaft. Note that the old tape is coming away too. This saves tedious scraping to remove old, hard tape.

Each shaft must be cleaned down to the bare metal. Go through your whole set, one club at a time, removing each old grip and preparing each shaft. Removing the grips and preparing the shafts is actually the major part of the regripping operation, because new grips go on very quickly and easily.

Putting on the New Grips

With each grip ordered, you receive one strip of golf shaft tape. This golf shaft tape, or double-stick tape, as it's called, is sticky on both sides, and each side is protected by a piece of release paper. When each shaft is clean and ready, you are ready to wind on the tape. Remove the release paper from one side and, starting at the butt end of the shaft, as shown in Photo 4-6, spiral wrap the strip of tape down the shaft, leaving approximately ⅛ inch of spacing between turns. Be sure to leave an overhang of about ¾ inch at the butt end of the shaft. Wrap the tape all the way down. Your 26-inch strip of double-stick tape will go down the length of the shaft—about 12 inches.

Now go back to the butt end of the shaft, where ¾ inch of tape

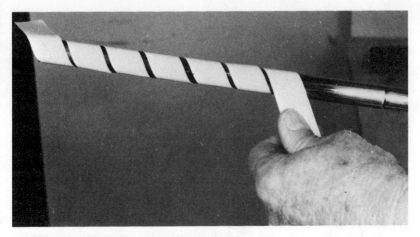

4-6. Wrapping the new tape: Leave about ¾ inch overhang at the butt end and spiral wrap the tape down the shaft. Fold the overhang over the open end of the shaft.

is overhanging. Pull off the outside layer of white release paper and fold the overhanging bit of tape over the open end of the shaft and down inside. What you're doing here is covering up the raw metal end of the shaft. If there is a burr or irregularity here, it may hook on the grip as you're installing it and stop your grip halfway down the shaft. But when you fold the tape over the end and inside the shaft, you protect against this problem.

The next step is wetting thoroughly the inside of the grip and the tape with a solvent such as paint thinner or mineral spirits. *Do this only in an open, well-ventilated space, well away from an open flame!* One of the handiest ways to wet down the tape and grip with solvent is to use an oilcan (see Photo 4-7).

Put the first grip in your left hand (right hand, if you are left-handed) and put your left forefinger over the small hole in the end cap of the grip. Now, with the oilcan in your right hand, squirt 2 or 3 tablespoons of paint thinner down the inside of this grip. Holding your left forefinger over the hole in the end cap, pinch the top end of the grip shut with your right thumb and forefinger. Next, shake the grip up and down a few times to wet its inside surface. Solvent makes the inside layer of the grip very

4-7. With an oil can containing solvent, squirt a couple of tablespoons inside the grip. Wet down the outside of tape on the shaft with solvent. Solvent makes the surfaces very slippery so that you can slide on the grip.

slippery, and when you wet the tape with solvent, the grip slides on easily.

Then dump out the solvent that is inside the grip. Take the oilcan in your free hand and go up and down the shaft a few times, putting a few drops of solvent every ½ to 1 inch for the full length of the tape. Then set down the oilcan and, with the new grip in your right hand, steady the shaft with your left hand. Line up the guideline or pattern on the grip with the hitting face of the club. The reminder feature inside the grip will automatically line up on the underside of the shaft. Pinch the opening of the grip together to get it started on the shaft, and then quickly slide the grip home until you feel it hit the end cap inside the grip.

4-8. Before the solvent can dry, pinch the open end of the grip, start the grip on the shaft, and shove it home. Line up the design with the lower edge of the hitting face.

Now the grip is installed. Take a look down the shaft to be sure that the pattern on the grip is lined up with the lower edge of the hitting face. If the center line on the grip is not perfectly lined up with the lower edge of the hitting face of the club, take the grip in both hands and twist it slightly in either direction until the pattern is lined up down the shaft.

Next, cut off any exposed tape with your razor blade or utility knife. If there is adhesive on the shaft, dampen a paper towel with a little paint thinner and wipe down the shaft.

Photo 4-9 shows the end result of regripping: a nice, fresh, clean, tacky golf grip that will help you hit straighter and harder and bring your score down a few strokes the first time you play with it.

4-9. The end result: fresh, clean, clinging golf grips that will help you hit straighter and save you strokes.

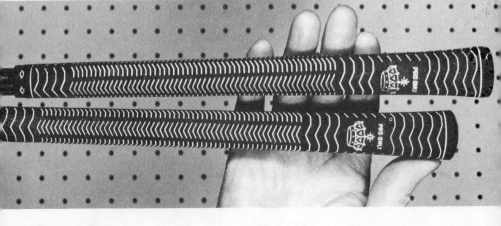

Installing Leather Grips

Follow these instructions for installing leather grips—either the slip-on or the wrap-on variety.

Slip-On Leather Grips

Slip-on leather grips are installed using the same method as that for rubber grips, with one exception: With leather grips, you must use a grip collar (Photo 4-10) to cover the raw edges of the leather at the bottom of the grip. A grip collar must be put on the shaft over the large or "butt" end with a small tool called a "starter" before you put on the grip. Press the end collar up and over the lower end of the leather grip and secure the collar with a spot of cement or epoxy.

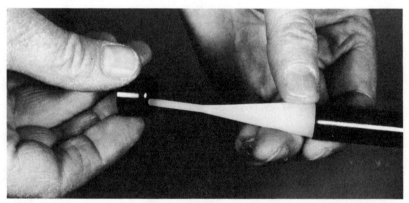

4-10. An end cap is necessary with any leather grip, whether it is a slip-on or a wrap-on grip. Using the white plastic starter as a guide, press the collar up and onto the shaft once the grip is in place.

Wrap-On Leather Grips

You will notice that, unlike a slip-on leather or plastic grip, a wrap-on leather grip comes in four pieces: two strips of tape, a leather wrap-on strip, and a floppy leather underlisting. The underlisting is a sort of liner with a built-in end cap that is installed on the shaft and then has leather wrapped around it.

To install a wrap-on leather grip, first remove the old grip and clean the shaft down to the bare metal. Put the grip collar on the shaft. Then wrap the butt end of the shaft with tape and install the rubber underlisting, using solvent on the tape and inside the underlisting.

With the rubber underlisting installed, you then must provide a base for the wrap-on leather strip. To do this, put one turn of golf grip tape around the end of the shaft, just beneath the end cap, as shown in Photo 4-11. Next, take the remainder of the second strip of tape and wrap it spirally down the shaft toward the head.

4-11. After the underlisting is installed, wrap one turn of tape around the end of the shaft, just under the end cap. Spiral wrap the remainder of the tape down the shaft.

Now you can start wrapping the leather. At the base of the end cap, there is a slight impression shaped like the cut end of the leather strip. Press the angle-cut tip of the leather strip in this impression to start the leather. (See Photo 4-12.) Pull the strip around and overlap the angle-cut end for about 1½ inches to help secure the top end of the leather strip. Then spiral wrap the leather strip down the shaft, over the tape on the underlisting, as shown in Photo 4-13. Overlap each turn between ⅟₁₆ and ⅛ inch, or you can butt the edges of the leather together.

When you get to the end of the leather strip, trim off this end so that it is square with the shaft. Holding the lower end of the leather wrap in place, press the end collar up and over the leather to hold it in position. Secure the collar with a few drops of model cement or epoxy and stand the club up on end for the epoxy to dry. The club is now regripped (Photo 4-14).

4-12. To start the leather strip, place the angle-cut end of the strip flush against the end cap as shown, and overlap the cut end with the first turn of the leather strip.

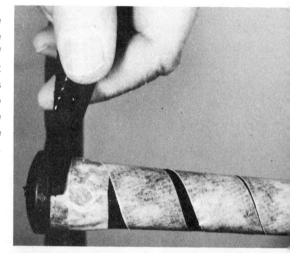

4-13. Using one hand to steady the work, pull the leather strip right and slightly overlap the leather with each turn. Wrap the leather strip over the tacky tape on down the shaft. Do not wet this tape with solvent.

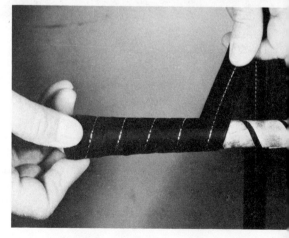

4-14. At the end of the leather, trim it square across with a razor blade and press the grip collar up and into position. Secure the collar with a few drops of model cement or epoxy.

INSTALLING CORD GRIPS

Cord grips are of the slip-on variety, and to put them on, follow the same procedure you would follow for installing rubber grips, using solvent and tape.

INSTALLING OVERSIZED GRIPS

Oversized grips are either procured by mail order or are made by converting regular rubber slip-on grips into oversized grips. Grips ordered by mail are slip-on grips and are installed just as rubber slip-on grips are.

To convert rubber grips, do it at the time the grip is installed. First, wrap one strip of tape around the shaft. Then wrap a second strip of tape around the shaft, so that there are two layers of tape all the way around the shaft. This provides a bigger base or foundation for the grip. Moisten the inside of the grip and the tape with solvent and slip the grip on. Two layers of tape are the limit because any more would make it very difficult to slip the grip on the shaft. Using this trick with extra tape, you can convert most of the popular rubber grips, such as the Green Victory, Men's Crown, Pro Plus Two, and the Silhouette grip, to oversized grips.

INSTALLING ARTHRITIC GRIPS

Arthritic grips are all rubber slip-on grips and are installed the same way as ordinary rubber slip-on grips. They are generally larger than average size, and have a molded shape to aid the arthritic golfer.

5
REFINISHING YOUR WOODS

After regripping, the most common golf club home repair job is refinishing woods. The thought of refinishing a set of wood clubs yourself may at first be overwhelming. The alternative to doing it yourself, however, is getting the clubs refinished at a pro shop or golf shop at a high cost of $12, $15, maybe even $18 per wood, whereas the do-it-yourself method will cost only about $2.00 or $2.50 per wood.

5-1. Examine wood heads regularly for signs of heavy wear and scuffing. When the surface is worn and broken, moisture can penetrate the wood.

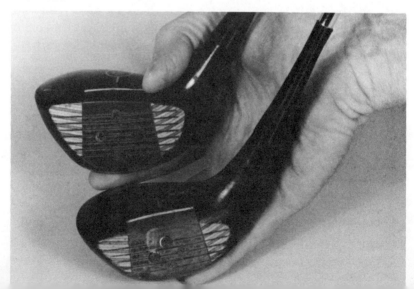

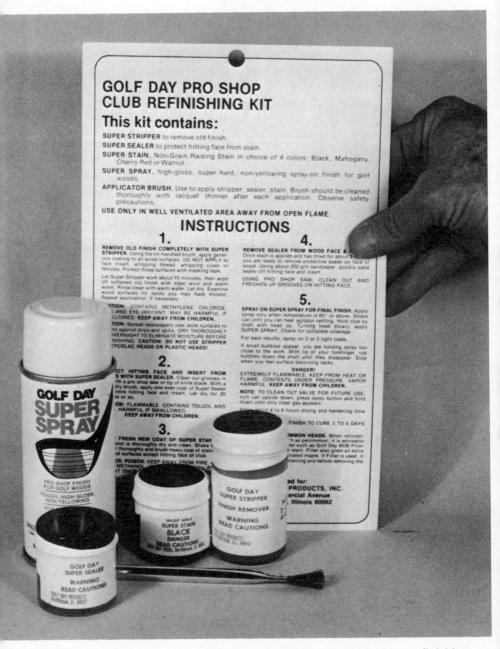

5-2. Golf wood refinishing kit has all the materials you need for basic refinishing.

Golfers who are unwilling to pay these prices have a low-cost option, for golf wood refinishing kits are now widely sold by mail. The kits come complete with clear, easy-to-read instructions and the materials necessary for doing a complete refinishing job on four to eight woods at home: a stripper to take off the old finish; a jar of sealer to seal off the hitting face; a jar of stain in a choice of several colors (black, cherry red, mahogany, walnut, and armour red); a spray can of high-gloss polyurethane finish. If you are refinishing persimmon woods, you also need a filler to apply on top of the stain. If a glossy, black, opaque finish is desired, you will need a spray can of black lacquer.

Add some masking tape, a cloth, and some extra-fine steel wool to the kit's materials and you are ready to begin refinishing.

HOW TO REFINISH WOODS

STRIPPING

The first step in refinishing is preparing the woods for the stripper. All inserts and whipping covers and/or whipping thread must be protected from the erosive action of the stripper. The easiest and best protection is masking tape, which should be laid over the insert with the straight side of the tape along the straight edge of the insert. Then masking tape should be wrapped around the whipping on the shaft to protect the whipping from the chemical action of the stripper (Photo 5-3).

Once the insert and whipping are protected, apply the stripper or finish remover (Photo 5-4). The refinishing kit includes a 2-ounce jar of stripper, enough to do four to eight woods. All exposed wood surfaces, including the hitting face and the sole plate, must be covered with stripper. After stripper is applied to the surface of a wood, let the stripper work for 25 minutes or so.

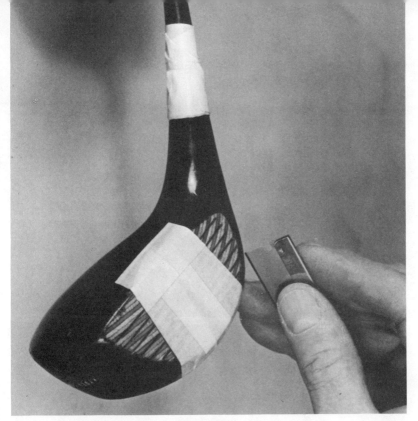

5-3. To prepare woods for removal of the old finish, protect the insert and whipping from action of the stripper by covering them with masking tape.

5-4. With a small brush, apply the stripper to all exposed wood surfaces and let it work for about 25 minutes.

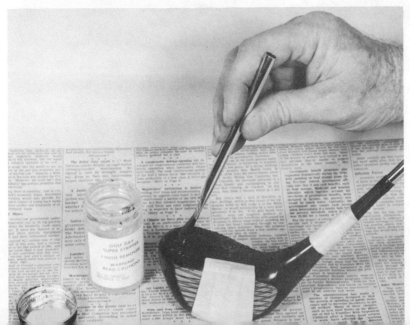

After 25 minutes, with a damp terry cloth towel or paper towels, wipe the stripper off all wood surfaces (Photo 5-5). Remove all of the stripper possible and then examine the wood closely to see if any glossy spots or slick places remain where the old finish has not been removed completely. Apply more stripper to any spots of finish remaining. When the head is finally clean, wash it down with a piece of rough terry cloth towel or a handful of wet paper towels. Be sure that all old finish and all finishing materials are removed. Let it dry overnight.

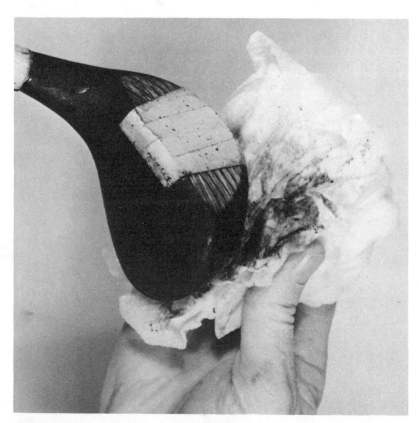

5-5. When the stripper has softened the old finish, remove it with a wet towel. Check the surface of the wood for spots of finish the stripper may have missed. Wash the head and let it dry overnight.

SEALING AND STAINING

When the head has dried, rub it down with 100 or 150 grit sandpaper and apply sealer to the hitting face. Sealer is necessary to protect the hitting face from drips and spills of stain that may occur during the staining process. Notice that in Photo 5-6 the wood appears quite dark although new stain has not yet been applied. That's because this head was finished in black and when the old finish was removed, the stain had penetrated into the wood and could not be removed without bleaching.

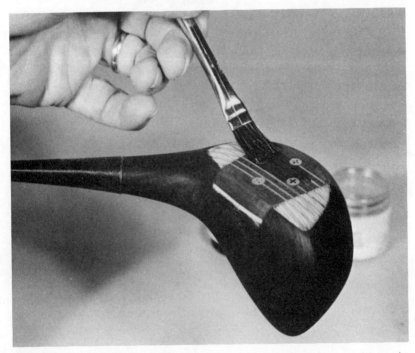

5-6. When the head has dried, treat the hitting face and insert with sealer to prevent the stain from penetrating.

The next step is applying stain to the stripped and washed head (Photo 5-7). Using the small brush and the small jar of stain in the refinishing kit, apply a new coat of stain to all the wood surfaces of the head—the top, sides, back, and sole area—except the hitting face. Let the stain dry for 30 minutes.

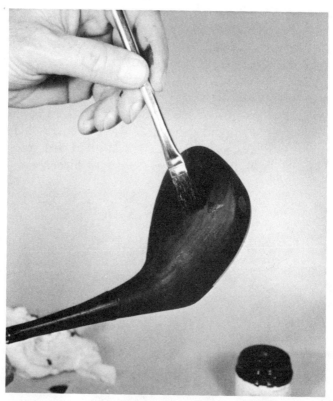

5-7. Apply new stain with the brush in the refinishing kit. When the stain has dried, remove the masking tape. Clean out grooves and cross slots in insert screws.

If you are refinishing persimmon heads, a filler should be used over the stain. Follow directions on the can and let it dry four hours.

FINISHING

Next, touch up the sole plate and wood screws before the final finish. Sand the sole plate to remove corrosion and chemical deposits that might have accumulated (Photo 5-8). If there is stain on the metal sole plate, remove it with a small swab dipped in rubbing alcohol.

The last step in the refinishing process is applying a hard-

surface, high-gloss polyurethane finish. Wipe off the head and
check for specks of dust. Hold the spray can 8 to 10 inches from
the wood and spray in short bursts. At this stage you must be
very careful to make sure that no sags and runs are caused by
excess spray. If small bubbles appear on the wood face surface,
touch them lightly with a finger and they will disappear
without a trace. Two or three light coats of polyurethane spray

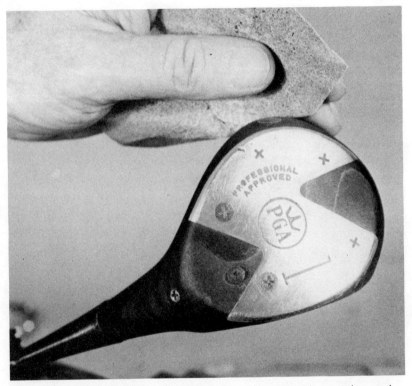

5-8. Sand the sole plate to remove any accumulated corrosion and
chemical deposits.

are better than one or two heavy coats. Let the first coat of spray
dry overnight and rub it down lightly with extra-fine steel wool
to remove any dust specks or blemishes. Apply a second coat, let
it dry overnight, and rub down with steel wool.

When the second coat of polyurethane spray has dried, apply

a replacement decal to the wood surface (Photo 5-9). Decals for all major brands of clubs are available and can be ordered by mail when you order your refinishing kit. Moisten the decal in a saucer of water and slip it into position on top of the wood head. Let the decal dry overnight, give the head one more light coat of spray finish to protect the decal, and let it dry for one more night. You now have a completely refinished golf club.

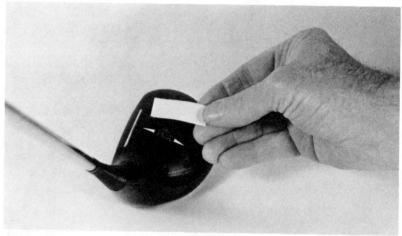

5-9. When the polyurethane spray finish has dried, apply a new decal.

6
WRAPPING WHIPPING THREAD

If there's anything that spoils a golfer's day, it's seeing that the whipping on a fine driver or a favorite fairway wood has suddenly broken and the whole thing is rapidly unwinding. It means a sure trip to the golf shop—unless you know how to wind the whipping yourself. If you occasionally refinish woods or customize unfinished woods, you will certainly find it very helpful to learn how to wrap your own whipping.

6-1. Tightly wrapped whipping thread is necessary to protect the neck of a fine wood. Whipping thread prevents the neck of the wood from splitting and cracking.

Bear in mind one firm rule about the whipping of woods: Never, never, never use a wood if the whipping is missing or coming unwound—not even one hit! Three or four hits on an unprotected neck of a wood are almost certain to split the wood, possibly beyond repair.

Learning to wind your own whipping is not difficult. Thousands of golfers do it every year and keep a hank of whipping thread on hand for emergency repairs. While not a big money saver, it certainly saves time.

6-2. Whipping a wood club is done much more easily with the help of a simple gadget that you can easily mount on your workbench. Go to a store that sells Polyvinyl Chloride Plastic (PVC) pipe and get a white PVC end cap and a large wood screw, as shown here.

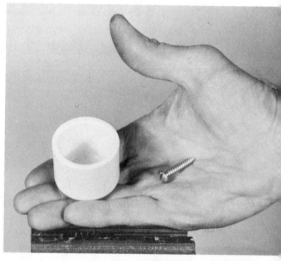

One simple gadget that's a tremendous help in winding whipping is shown in Photo 6-3. It's nothing more than a PCV pipe end cap secured to the back of a workbench with a good-sized wood screw. This end cap holds the butt end of the shaft firm and keeps it under control while you are winding the whipping with your two hands.

6-3. Drill a hole through the end of the PVC cap and mount it on the back wall of your workbench. The grip of the club you are about to whip will fit in here, and the end cap will keep the club secure while you are wrapping the whipping.

To start your whipping, with a small brush paint a streak of shellac down the underside of the ferrule and onto the neck. Place the loose end of whipping into this sticky shellac and wind over it with about 10 turns, as shown in Figure 6-A.

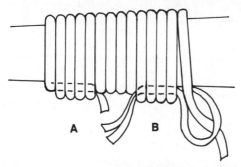

6-A (above, left). Start your new whipping near the top of the ferrule on the shaft of the wood. Lay about ¾ inch of whipping down the underside of the ferrule. Wrap over this loose end of whipping, and wrap on down the shaft getting tight, even turns by using the procedure shown in Photo 6-4. Wrap whipping evenly down the neck of the wood to a point at about 2½ inches above the heel of the club. 6-B (above, right). To tie the whipping use either this method or the method illustrated in Figure 6-C. To tie the whipping as shown here, lay a double loop of whipping thread along the shaft and wrap over it for about six or eight turns. Put the lower end of the whipping through this loop and draw the loop out, bringing the end of the whipping with it. Pull tight and seal with shellac.

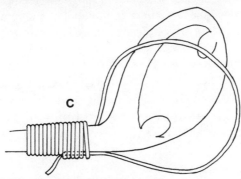

6-C. The second and more preferred method of tying off whipping is shown here. When you are ready to tie the whipping, lay out a big loop of whipping thread, bring the free end back up and along the underside of the shaft, and throw six or eight loops over it. Pull the free end of the loop tight, and then trim off excess whipping thread with a razor blade or nail cutters.

With the butt of the grip rotating in the pipe end cap and your left elbow holding the shaft firmly against your hip, play out the thread between your left thumb and forefinger as your right rotates the club head (Photo 6-4). After 100 to 115 turns, prepare to tie the knot with one of two methods—either the method shown in Figure 6-B or the method shown in Figure 6-C.

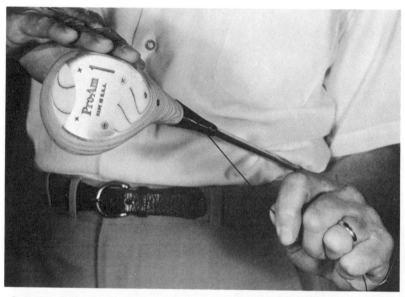

6-4. Winding the whipping: With the end of the grip in the white end cap, hold the shaft against your left hip with your left elbow. Play out the thread between the left thumb and forefinger and rotate the head with the right hand for a nice, neat winding.

Once you have whipped a club or two, you will quickly get the hang of it and do as good a job as a neighborhood golf shop would. And think of the time you can save (time you can be on the golf course) by wrapping your whipping thread at home in a few minutes instead of sending your club to the shop for a week or two.

7

CHECKING AND CHANGING BULGE AND ROLL FOR BETTER WOOD SHOTS

Bulge and roll are found on the hitting face of all really well-made wood clubs. Bulge is the convex curvature of the hitting face as measured from side to side; roll is the convex curvature of the hitting face as measured from top to bottom.

Golf club designers say that bulge and roll help you get straighter hits and better carry, even if you don't hit quite squarely. They also say that a design with bulge and roll is "more forgiving" than a design with a perfectly flat hitting face. With a wood that has bulge and roll, the ball makes contact at only one point of a rounded surface; therefore, you get a spin that minimizes air resistance and helps you get the extra distance.

Bulge and roll come in four different degrees of curvature—that with an 8-inch radius, a 10-inch radius, a 12-inch radius, and a 14-inch radius. The 10-inch radius, as seen in Photo 7-1, is most common.

7-1. Measuring roll. Roll is a convex curvature of the hitting face measured from top to bottom.

MEASURING BULGE AND ROLL

If you are not getting quite the hits with your wood clubs that you would like, it is worth checking the clubs' bulge and roll. Bulge and roll are checked with a golf club face radius gauge, as shown in Photos 7-2 and 7-3. The gauge is inexpensive and easy to use.

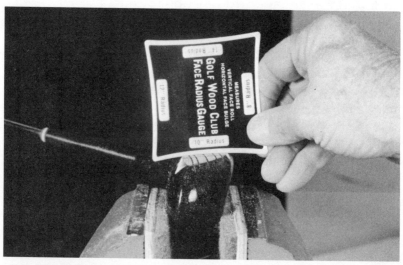

7-2. Bulge and roll are measured with a face radius gauge.

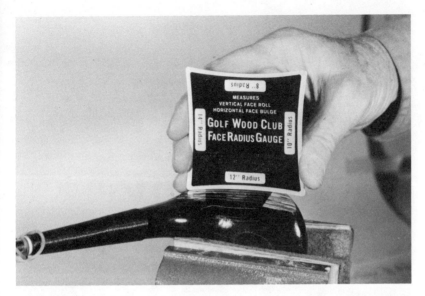

7-3. Measuring bulge. Bulge is a convex curvature of the hitting face measured from side to side.

ALTERING BULGE AND ROLL

It is also easy to change bulge and roll. Use a flat mill file that is fairly coarse to remove a little wood from top to bottom and from side to side (Photo 7-4). File the wood away very carefully and check the hitting face frequently with your face radius gauge, because once the wood is filed away, it cannot be put back. In addition, you can add a bit of hook or slice to the hitting face of the wood (see Chapter 2) when you are adjusting bulge and roll.

When the radius of the wood is down to the figure you want, it is a simple matter to dust off the club and seal its hitting face with a couple of coats of polyurethane from a spray can.

7-4. Remove a little wood with a coarse file to change bulge and roll.

8
REPLACING HITTING-FACE INSERTS

Sooner or later you will find it necessary to replace the face insert in a club to save a favorite set of woods. Naturally, the inserts of the fairway woods, the 3, 4, and 5 woods, are damaged most frequently. (The damaged insert in Photo 8-1 is in a 3 wood.) When hitting off thin fairway grass, the wood head frequently makes contact with the ground. If the soil contains small pebbles or stone fragments, you are certain to have a scarred and battered insert after a season or two of play.

Whether the insert is of standard or odd size, you can save time and money by replacing it yourself.

8-1. This scarred and dented insert needs replacing. The clear epoxy inlay is cracked.

REPLACING STANDARD INSERTS

Standard-sized replacement inserts can be ordered by mail or sometimes bought at a golf shop. The first step in replacing a standard insert is removing the sole plate so that you can get at the bottom of the insert where it joins the wood. Remove the screws and mark each one so that each screw can be returned to the same screw hole (Photo 8-2). When the screws are removed, take a thin strong chisel, such as a golf wood insert chisel, and tap it in the joint between the insert and the sole plate. If the sole plate has not been cemented down with epoxy, it will lift off very easily, as is shown in Photo 8-3.

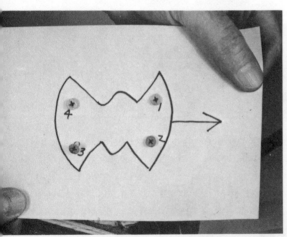

8-2. The first step is to remove the sole plate so we can get at the insert from underneath. Loosen the screws in turn. Identify each sole plate screw so it can be replaced in the same screw hole.

8-3. Now that the screws are removed, lift off the sole plate with a thin chisel.

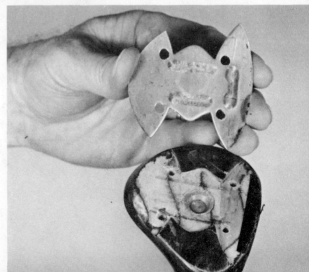

The next step is removing the old, battered insert. First try tapping it a few times with the sole plate chisel where the insert joins the wood under the sole plate. Sometimes an insert will pop right out if the epoxy is dry and brittle.

8-4. Using the thin insert chisel, tap the insert where it joins the wood to see if you can pop it out.

If the insert will not pop out in one piece, a little more effort is required. With the head securely locked in a bench vise between felt pads, take a hacksaw and carefully cut through the insert top to bottom in about three or four places, as shown in Photo 8-5. Be very careful to cut only the insert material and not

8-5. When the insert will not pop out in one piece, it is necessary to make several cuts from top to bottom and remove it in pieces.

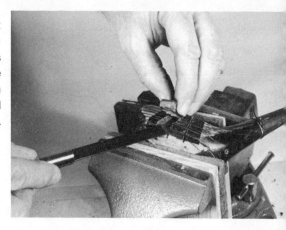

into the wood. If you cut too deeply at the top of the insert, you are going to mar the wood where it can be seen. When three cuts have been made in the insert from top to bottom, tap the insert chisel underneath each section of insert in turn. Each piece of insert should then lift out neatly. When pieces of insert have been removed from the insert cavity, with a coarse mill file remove any fragments of dried epoxy or splinters of wood that would prevent the new insert from seating completely.

Slip the new insert into the insert cavity to make sure that it seats properly. Since the insert is narrower at the top than it is at the bottom, press the insert to the top of the wood head to wedge it in securely. Now check it for a tight fit all around. If it's too large, remove excess material with a file. If the insert makes good contact with the wood on each side of the shaft cavity, you are ready to epoxy the new insert in place.

The best epoxy for securing a new insert is regular golf shaft epoxy, which has high-impact, high-shock qualities. Using a wood coffee stirrer, mix the parts of the golf shaft epoxy on a one-to-one ratio in a disposable paper plate or dish. Coat the insert cavity thoroughly with the epoxy mixture to ensure a good bond (Photo 8-6).

8-6. Spread epoxy on the sides and back of the insert cavity with a flat, wooden stir stick.

Then coat the back and sides of the new insert with golf shaft epoxy so that two epoxied surfaces will come together. Slip the new insert into place and wedge it to the top as tightly as possible (Photo 8-7). Then take two or three heavy rubber bands

8-7. Coat the back and sides of the new insert liberally with golf shaft epoxy and slip it into the cavity.

and snap them around the insert and the wood head to keep the pressure on toward the top of the cavity (Photo 8-8). The next day or so, when the epoxy has had plenty of time to set, remove the rubber bands and test the new insert with your fingers to make sure that it is securely cemented into the cavity.

8-8. While the epoxy is drying, fasten the insert in place with heavy rubber bands to keep the pressure on it. Next day, test the insert to see if it is secure.

The next step is to file and grind the new insert down flush with the wood top and bottom. For the first part of this process, you can use a small grinder on a hand-held electric drill. But be careful, because if you take off too much insert material then there's no other solution than knocking this new insert out and putting in a new one.

In Photo 8-9, a file is being used to file the insert flush with the wood under the sole plate. Remember that the sole plate is slightly curved, and your insert should therefore be filed with a slight curve so that the metal sole plate will fit it exactly. Replace the sole plate and return each sole plate screw to its original screw hole.

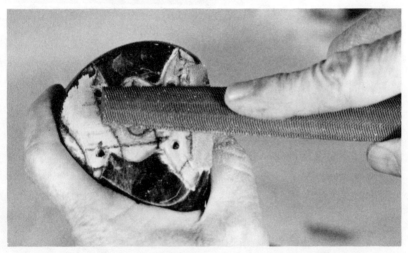

8-9. Overhanging insert material is removed by filing. As you remove insert material be careful not to nick the surface of the wood.

The next steps are sanding the insert face flush with the wood on the hitting face (Photo 8-10) and cutting new grooves to line up with the grooves in the wood face. To cut new grooves be sure to use a no-set saw blade. When the new grooves are completed and the insert sanded (Photo 8-11), spray the hitting face with two or three coats of clear polyurethane finish. Let the finish cure for three or four days. Then you will be ready to put the club back in your bag and take it out on the golf course.

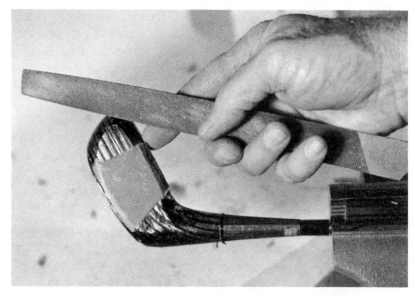

8-10. Sand the insert flush with the wood of the hitting face.

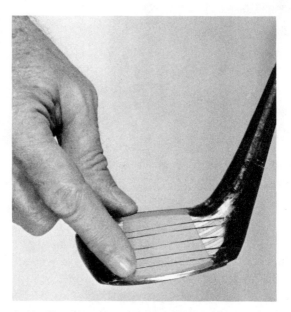

8-11. The insert has been sanded flush with the wood and new grooves have been cut.

POUR-IN-PLACE EPOXY INSERTS

With several dozen golf club makers turning out millions of woods every year, many of them new designs, inserts come in a great variety of shapes and sizes. There are extra-wide inserts, tapered inserts, thick inserts, inserts that are square without a taper, oval-shaped inserts, and narrow inserts. When you have a broken insert that is not of standard shape or size, the best solution is what the trade calls a *pour-in-place epoxy insert.* Liquid epoxy material is poured into an insert cavity of any size or shape, and it hardens to form a new insert. You probably won't find it in golf shops or pro shops, but it is available by mail. Such inserts are usually available in red or black.

Pour-in-place epoxy inserts come in two plastic jars. Both part A and part B are liquid until mixed together. They then set hard in about 24 hours to form a new insert that conforms exactly to the size and shape of the insert cavity.

To replace a battered insert with pour-in-place epoxy insert material, first remove the old insert and clean out the insert cavity. It's a good idea to rough up the bottom and sides of the insert cavity with a coarse file, so that the epoxy material has a good surface to bond onto.

Lock the head in a vise between felt pads with the hitting face up (Photo 8-12). The next step is to build a dam or container for

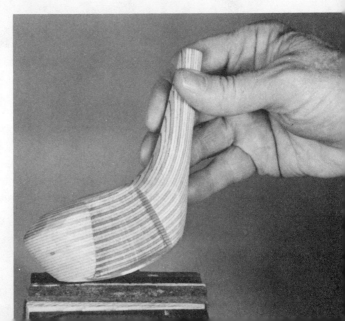

8-12. With old inserts removed, lock the head in a vise between felt pads with the hitting face up.

the epoxy insert material. Using strips of caulking putty, as shown in Photo 8-13, build a little square box or dam around the cavity to contain the liquid epoxy. Be sure that you build this box high enough. Remember that the leading edge of the sole plate has a curve to it; it's higher in the center than it is at the side, so you must build your dam or box high enough for the epoxy to cover this high spot.

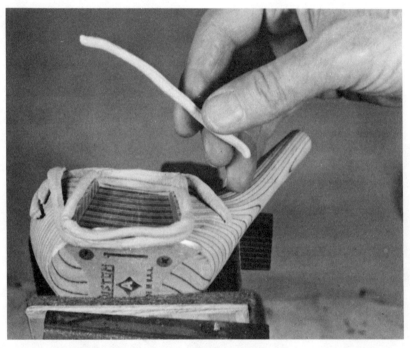

8-13. Use strips of caulking putty to build a dam to contain the epoxy insert material.

Next, mix up the epoxy by pouring equal parts of part A and part B epoxy into a disposable paper mixing dish and stir thoroughly with a wooden coffee stirring stick (Photo 8-14). Be sure that the head is absolutely level in the vise on your workbench. When you have the head and the dam level, pour in enough epoxy to cover the leading edge of the sole plate and also the wood sides of the head (Photo 8-15).

8-14. Mix parts A and B of epoxy insert material at a one-to-one ratio in a disposable paper dish.

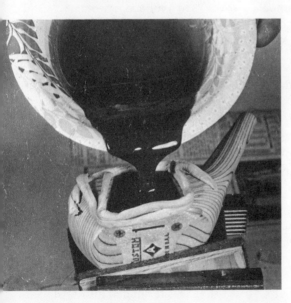

8-15. Level the head in your bench vise, and fill the insert cavity with the epoxy.

Leave the head in the vise on your workbench in a level position for one or two days, until the epoxy has had enough time to set completely. The warmer the temperature, the faster the epoxy will set. If your work area is located in an unheated area of the house, hang a heat lamp or a 100-watt bulb over the epoxy to give it enough heat for a fast cure. When the epoxy material has cured, remove the head from the vise (Photo 8-16).

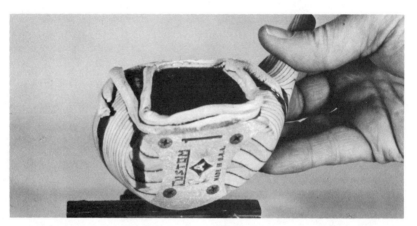

8-16. Cure in a warm place (over 75° F.) for about two days. Remove caulking cord, sand the new insert flush, and cut new grooves with a no-set saw blade.

From this point on, follow the same procedure as that for finishing off a standard-sized replacement insert. Remove the caulking cord, and sand the insert material flush with the wood of the hitting face.

Notice that in Photo 8-16 some of the epoxy escaped where the caulking cord was not pressed tightly enough against the wood. If this happens, remove the escaped epoxy with a sanding tool after it is cured. When you have sanded the new epoxy insert flush with the wood, use a no-set saw blade to cut new grooves in the insert matching those in the wood on each side.

You will find that your club with the new epoxy insert has first-class hitting qualities. Many golfers say that they get a better distance from a pour-in-place epoxy insert than they did from the original cycolac insert that was damaged and replaced.

9
SHAFTS
TYPES OF SHAFTS, INSTALLING SHAFTS, AND SHAFT EXTENDERS

Both woods and irons have *shafts,* the tubes that connect the head and the grip of a golf club. This chapter discusses shafts in general and then explains how to replace a broken shaft, how to lengthen a club with a shaft extender, and how to ream out a wood head to fit a larger shaft—all jobs that you can do yourself.

CHARACTERISTICS OF SHAFTS

In recent years, some very high-performance shafts that offer light weight, strength, and excellent performance have come on the scene—those made of graphite fibers, fiberglass, lightweight steel, chrome, vanadium steel, and other unique materials. In addition, of course, a few hickory putters are still on the market.

Most shafts, however, are made of steel. Steel shafts come in a variety of flexes, tip and butt sizes, and lengths.

FLEXES

You might describe *flex* as a varying degree of flexibility or whip built into the various types of shafts. Generally speaking, the less muscle the golfer has, the more whip should be built into the shaft; and the more muscular the golfer, the more stiffness the golfer can handle in a shaft.

Shafts for both iron and wood clubs are made in five flexes. There's a ladies' flex shaft, an "A" flex shaft for senior golfers, an "R" or regular flex shaft for the average hitter, an "S" or stiff flex shaft for the good, strong hitters, and an "X" or extra-stiff flex shaft for the very muscular, long-distance hitters.

TIP SIZES

Tip sizes are measured in one-thousandths of an inch. So a tip size of .277 means it is 277/1000 inch. The tip size of a shaft must match exactly the tip size that the head is bored for.

Wood heads are commonly bored for a tip size of .277, .294, or .335. The common tip sizes for irons are .355 and .370. The .355 tip, the most common, is a taper tip for irons; the .370 shaft is a parallel or straight tip for irons.

Another type of shaft for irons is the over-the-hosel shaft. Instead of a hosel that is bored out to take a shaft, the neck is a solid spindle with an outer diameter of .355. To shaft a head, the spindle is painted with epoxy, and a shaft with an inner diameter of .355 slips down or is driven down over it.

SHAFT LENGTHS

Most wood shafts come in a basic 44-inch length. One inch is trimmed off the butt, or big end, to get a 43-inch shaft, which is the usual length of a driver. Use the following table to trim the shafts of wood clubs to the correct length.

GOLF WOOD FITTING TABLE

If Driver is 43", then . . .

2-wood is 42½"	6-wood is 40¾"
3-wood is 42"	7-wood is 40½"
4-wood is 41½"	8-wood is 40⅜"
5-wood is 41"	9-wood is 40¼"

Iron shafts usually come in four basic lengths: 35, 36, 37, and 38 inches. If you want a 35-inch 9 iron, for instance, then install a 35-inch shaft, measure the distance from heel to butt, and cut off the excess length to end up with a 35-inch 9 iron. Use the following table to trim the shaft of iron clubs to the correct length.

GOLF IRON FITTING TABLE

If 2-iron is 38½", then . . .

3-iron is 38″	Chipping iron is 36″
4-iron is 37½″	7-iron is 36″
5-iron is 37″	8-iron is 35½″
6-iron is 36½″	9-iron is 35″
	PW/SW is 35″

A golf shaft cutter (Photo 9-1) is a basic tool for trimming a shaft. A hacksaw will do just fine, but it's slower.

9-1. Golf shaft cutter

INSTALLING A SHAFT

Sooner or later, you'll need to have a new golf shaft installed. Maybe you'll need to replace a shaft that was broken when it got caught in a car trunk door or when your golf bag was run over by somebody's golf cart. Or maybe you'll just want to change all of your irons from regular-flex shafts to stiff-flex shafts.

For whatever reason, the job will get done much more quickly and inexpensively if you just do it yourself. With a few simple tools replacing a shaft of any wood or iron club is a small job any golfer can do in 15 minutes or so. All you need is the new shaft, a rubber vise clamp, a heavy cotton work glove for your left hand (right hand, if you're left-handed), and a *small* torch. (With a large torch, you're more likely to turn the shaft cherry red in about 20 seconds, which destroys the temper and ruins the shaft.)

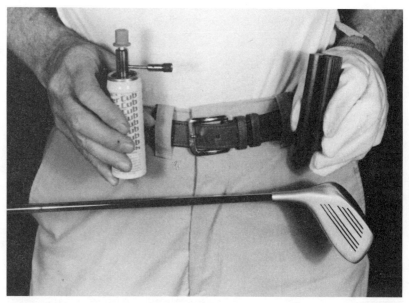

9-2. Tools needed to replace a broken golf shaft: a small torch to soften the epoxy, a vise clamp, and a cotton glove.

When you order a replacement shaft or a new set of shafts by mail, either for woods or irons, it is essential that you order the correct tip size. To prevent confusion, either measure the tip size with a micrometer or send in the actual broken tip for the company to match. Don't expect replacement shafts to match the old shafts exactly, especially if you play with name-brand woods and irons. The big manufacturers often have their shafts made up with their own exclusive step patterns, and no one else has a right to buy these shafts.

REMOVING THE OLD SHAFT

Irons and Metal-Headed Woods

For any iron club or any wood club with a metal head, follow these instructions for removing the old shaft. In Photos 9-3 and 9-4, a Unitized Dynamic shaft is being removed from a metal wood head to be replaced by a Dynamic shaft with a reinforced tip.

After locking the club in a bench vise at a good working angle, apply heat from a small torch directly to the shaft, just above the hosel of the club head (Photo 9-3). The heat travels down the

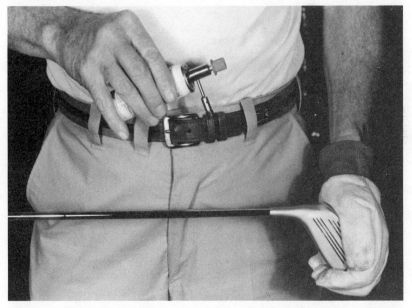

9-3. Turn on the flame and aim direct heat from the torch on the shaft an inch or so above the hosel. After a couple of minutes, give the head a twist.

shaft inside the hosel and softens the epoxy, so that you can twist off the head with your gloved hand (Photo 9-4).

When removing a shaft from an iron club, many pros advise applying heat from the torch directly on the hosel. This softens the epoxy but may discolor the hosel of the iron.

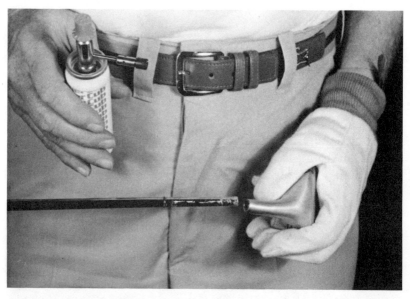

9-4. When heat softens the epoxy, you can twist the head right off. Clean charred epoxy out of the shaft cavity.

Wood-Headed Woods

When the club has a wood head, protect its finish by covering it with aluminum foil (Photo 9-5).

Always check the back of a wood head about an inch above the heel for a backscrew, called a *pin*.

If the wood head does not have a pin, the procedure for removing the old shaft is the same as that described above for irons and metal-headed woods—except that you must allow more time for the heat to travel down the shaft, since there are approximately 4 inches of shaft in some woods and only 1½ inches of shaft in woods with metal heads.

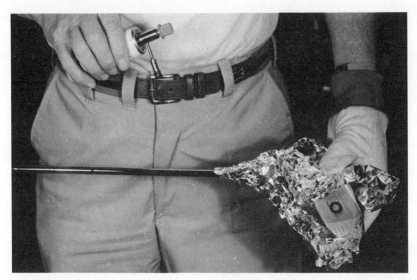

9-5. After turning on the torch, protect the finish on a wood head with a piece of aluminum foil.

If the wood head *is* pinned onto the shaft, however, then you must cut the pin before the head can come free (Photo 9-6). If the shaft is drilled through the wood of the sole, then go up the

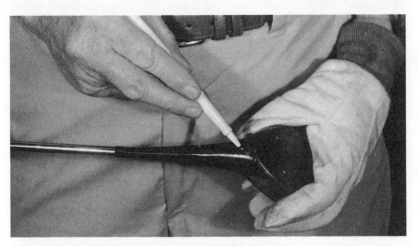

9-6. If wood head is pinned to the shaft, you must remove this pin or backscrew before the head will come off.

inside of the shaft from the bottom with a ¼-inch drill. Cut the pin and draw out the head of the pin. If the shaft does not extend through the hole, you must remove the grip (see Chapter 4) and go down the shaft from the top with a long 48-inch drill to cut the pin. After removing the outer head of the pin, slip a small punch in the hole and drive the inner tip of the pin further into the wood. Then apply heat and the shaft should come free.

REPLACING THE SHAFT

Once the old shaft is removed, clean the charred epoxy out of the shaft cavity and blow it clean. Rough up the tip of the new shaft with sandpaper, coat it with epoxy, slip it into the old head, and leave it standing upright overnight for the epoxy to set. The next day, trim to length and install the grip.

LENGTHENING CLUBS WITH SHAFT EXTENDERS

If you are a taller-than-average golfer, regular golf clubs may seem a little short for you. Since clubs are designed for a golfer of average height—from around 5 feet 10 inches to 6 feet—you may wish for a simple and inexpensive way to lengthen your favorite clubs.

Golf repair shops use a segment of steel tubing called a *shaft extender* to add ½ to 3 inches or more to the butt end of a shaft. Not often found on sale to the general public, extenders are available through mail order in the three principal golf shaft diameters, .580, .600, and .620 inch. By doing the job yourself, you will save not only time, but three-quarters of the pro shop cost.

To ensure that you order shaft extenders with the correct diameter, remove an old grip (as shown in Photo 9-7 and described in Chapter 4) and check the butt size with a micrometer (Photo 9-8) or a golf shaft butt gauge (Photo 9-9) to get the exact measurement.

When you receive your golf shaft extenders, it will be clear

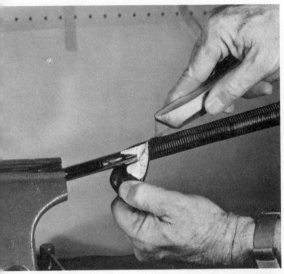

9-7. A golf club is lengthened at the butt or grip end. First, remove the old grip.

9-8. Measure the size of the shaft exactly, as with a micrometer here. It may be .580, .600, or .620 inch. You must know the size to order and install the right shaft extender.

9-9. Or, you can measure the butt size of the shaft with a grip and shaft gauge. This gauge will give you almost as accurate a measurement as a micrometer.

how they work. Each extender has a step-down portion that slides into the butt of the shaft and is secured with epoxy. To check the size of the extenders, lock the shaft in a vise at a good working angle and slip the step-down portion of a shaft extender into the open (butt) end of the shaft (Photos 9-10 and 9-11). It should be a rather close fit and should slide in with only a little pressure. If the extender wobbles around, it is too loose and you probably need the next larger size.

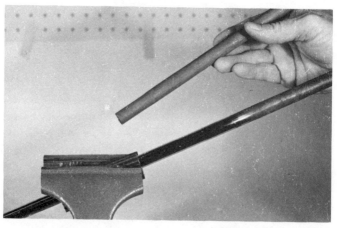

9-10. Lock the shaft in a vise, using a vise clamp, at a good working angle as shown here. Note that the shaft extender has a slight step-down shoulder.

9-11. Test the shaft extender in the open butt end of the shaft for size. It should fit very closely.

When you know that the shaft extender is the right size, rough up its tip with sandpaper to provide a good grabbing surface for the epoxy. Mix up a tablespoon or so of golf shaft epoxy and thoroughly coat the step-down portion of the shaft extender. Slip it inside the open end of the shaft and twirl it around to ensure that the epoxy is well distributed. Then apply more epoxy to the tip, slip it into the shaft, and stand the club upright overnight to cure.

The next day, when the epoxy has set, trim off the excess length of the shaft extender to give you exactly the desired overall shaft length. In Photo 9-12, for example, exactly 2 inches of shaft length have been added by using a shaft extender. When the shaft is the length you want, wrap it with golf grip tape and install your favorite golf grip, as discussed in Chapter 4.

With golf shafts that are cut to the right length for your height, you will certainly play a better game.

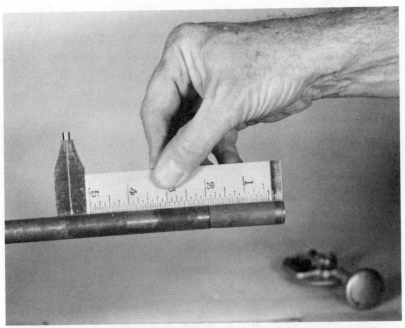

9-12. The finished job. This shaft extender lengthens the shaft by exactly 2 inches. Now wrap with tape and install a new grip.

REAMING OUT A WOOD HEAD FOR A LARGER SHAFT

When working with wood golf clubs, it is occasionally necessary or desirable to increase the size of the shaft cavity that is already bored into the neck of a wood head so it will take a larger size shaft.

In Photos 9-13 to 9-16, an unfinished laminated maple wood head that is already bored for a shaft with a tapered .294 tip is being reamed out so that it will take a Unitized shaft with a .335 parallel tip. When the wood remaining outside the current shaft cavity is as thick as it is in this head, it is no great trick to drill out the shaft cavity so that it will take a larger shaft. When working with a fine persimmon head or a finished maple head where the wall of its neck is very thin, however, it is not advisable to try to enlarge the shaft cavity because you are almost certain to split the wood.

To prepare the wood head for enlarging the shaft cavity, lock the head in a bench vise at a good working angle, using your heavy felt vise pads (Photo 9-13). Then protect the neck of the head against splitting by wrapping it tightly with several turns of ordinary masking tape (Photo 9-14) or with 15 to 20 turns of whipping thread.

9-13. To ream out a wood so that a larger shaft can be installed, lock the wood head in your bench vise using the thick felt vise pads.

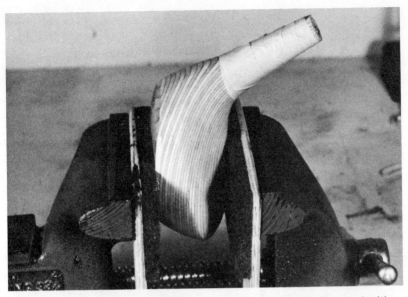

9-14. Protect the wood against splitting by wrapping the hosel with several turns of masking tape or whipping thread.

To ensure that you don't drill too deeply and have the drill go through the sole of the wood head, wrap a band of masking tape around the drill bit to mark the desired depth of the shaft cavity, as in Photo 9-15. This simple safeguard can prevent a ruined head.

9-15. To ensure that the drill bit or reamer does not go through the sole of the wood, mark the proper distance on the drill bit with a band of masking tape. Here, the drill bit will go within ⅜ inch of the sole of the wood head.

Next, lock the drill bit in a ⅜-inch drill and carefully ream out the wood to the desired depth (Photo 9-16). Laminated maple is extremely hard, and the drill bit may soon overheat if you try to drill too fast. Therefore, it is advisable to drill in short bursts.

The whole drilling operation takes only a minute or two. When the drilling is done, test a shaft of the desired size in the shaft cavity to see that it will seat to the desired depth. When the shaft cavity is correct, remove the masking tape from around the neck of the wood and proceed to the next step of installing the shaft.

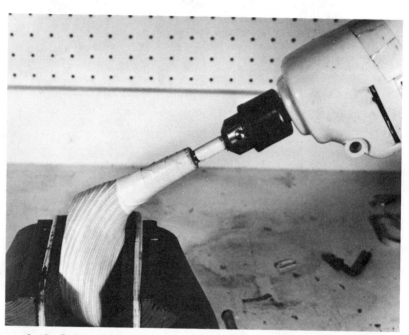

9-16. Center the drill bit on the hole that's already bored and then carefully drill out the shaft cavity to the desired depth.

10
CHECKING AND CHANGING SWING WEIGHT

Swing weighting, to put it in layperson's terms, means bringing all the clubs in a set into the same swinging balance. That means that a 2 iron, with its long shaft and lighter head, would have the same swinging balance or feel as the 9 iron, with its much shorter shaft and heavier head.

Swing weighting your set of clubs can improve your golf game. Low-handicap golfers pride themselves on having a swing that's "in the groove"; they have the same smooth, consistent swing with every club in their bags. To maintain that consistency, all of their clubs must have the same swing weight.

To aid bringing every golf club in a set to the same swing weight, golf club makers and fitters have developed a simple tool known as the *swing weight scale.* For many years after World War II, the standard of the industry was a swing weight scale made by the Kenneth Smith Company of Kansas City. A rather heavy, bench-type scale, it was best suited for use at a clubhouse.

75

Then, in the early '70s, the Karsten Manufacturing Company of Arizona developed the Ping swing weight scale (Photo 10-1), which has a good reputation for accuracy and many benefits not associated with a heavier, more cumbersome scale. The compact unit, measuring 22 inches long by 2 inches wide by 3½ inches high, can fit into a suitcase, a car trunk, or even a large pocket on a golf bag. (I've been told that some professional players carry a Ping scale with them on tour and that they may check the swing weight of their clubs once or twice during a tournament.) The scale is relatively inexpensive (one-quarter of the cost of big shop models), and easy to set up and read.

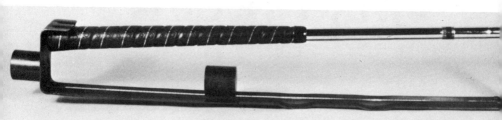

10-1. The Ping swing weight scale is portable, reliable, and easy to use.

To check a club's swing weight, the club is slipped over the support at the right end of the scale and under the bracket at the left. In the center is a sliding weight, which travels along a measuring tape or scale that is fastened to the lower bar. When the club is put on the scale, the weight is moved until the scale comes to a balance. Then the swing weight reading, on the right side of the weight, is taken (Photo 10-2). For an accurate reading, the table top must be level.

Swing weight is measured in points. The lightest clubs are lettered C, with numbers from 0 through 9; medium are D, 0 through 9; and the heaviest clubs are E, 0 through 9. The swing weight of most men's clubs falls in the range of D-0 to D-6. The swing weight of ladies' clubs falls in a range from C-5 to D-0 on a 10-point scale.

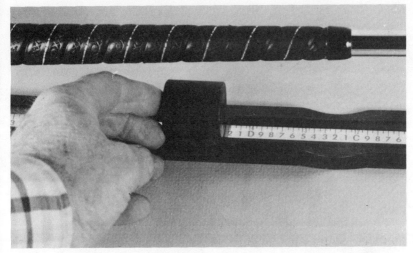

10-2. To get the swing weight of the club, the operator is sliding the scale's weight back and forth. When the beam comes to a balance, the reading will be on the right side of the weight.

IRONS

CHECKING SWING WEIGHT

To check the swing weight of a set of iron clubs, start with the longest iron in your bag—maybe a 2 or a 3 iron. Place the butt end (the grip end) of the club under the bracket on the left and the shaft of the club on the bracket on the right. Slide the weight up and down the bottom beam of the scale until it is in balance. Take a swing weight reading directly off the right side of the weight. You may get a D-1, D-1½, or D-2 reading. Run through all the clubs in your bag, recording the swing weight reading of each club on a sheet of paper in order to discover any variance in swing weights.

Let's say that your set of irons swing weights nicely at a reading of D-1, but your 5 iron is light, with a reading of C-9 or D-0. In such a case, you would perhaps want to add a little swing weight to that 5 iron.

CHANGING SWING WEIGHT

Because iron clubs have no sole plates, bringing an iron club into balance with the other irons is more difficult than bringing a wood into balance with the other woods. Generally, there are just two ways to alter the swing weight of an iron club.

The simpler, and therefore preferable, method of adding swing weight to an iron is to add lead tape across the back side of the blade opposite the hitting face.* Lead tape is sold by golf suppliers, and one 3-foot roll is enough to adjust the swing weight of several sets of clubs. As a general rule, 1 inch of lead tape will add approximately 1 point of swing weight to an iron club.

The other way to change an iron's swing weight involves a method commonly used in golf club manufacturing. Clubs are commonly manufactured a little on the light side, and when they are checked, extra weight is pressed down the shaft with a long rod before the grip is installed. Once lead weight has been installed in the shaft, it is not easily accessible. Thus, if an iron's swing weight is not accurate, it is necessary to remove the grip and fish around with a long steel drill to remove weight. To add weight, remove the grip and drop sections of lead wire down the shaft. Tap them in place with a steel rod and secure with a dab of epoxy.

WOODS WITH WOOD HEADS

CHECKING SWING WEIGHT

Check the swing weight of wood clubs just as you would that of irons. Beginning by swing weighing the lightest wood (the driver), record the swing weight reading of all the woods.

---

*Of course, the lead tape method is of no use to *subtracting* from a club's swing weight.

Changing Swing Weight

You can add to the swing weight of a wood club using the lead tape method, pressing the tape on the bottom of the sole plate or on the back of the head. You can add a piece of lead wire down the shaft, but this involves removing the grip.

The third way to alter the swing weight of a wood—to either increase or decrease it—is to take off the sole plate and add to or subtract from the lead weight that is underneath the sole plate. The steps to removing the sole place, altering the lead weight, and replacing the sole plate are detailed in Photos 10-3 through 10-11.

By adding weight to wood clubs that are too light for your muscular build or by lightening overly heavy wood clubs, you will find that you are getting wood shots that are a bit longer and straighter. And the best way to change the head weight of woods is to adjust the weight under the sole plate.

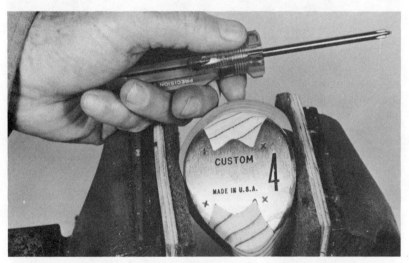

10-3. The first step to removing the sole plate is securing the wood head in a bench vise, using vise pads on each side to protect it from the jaws of the vise.

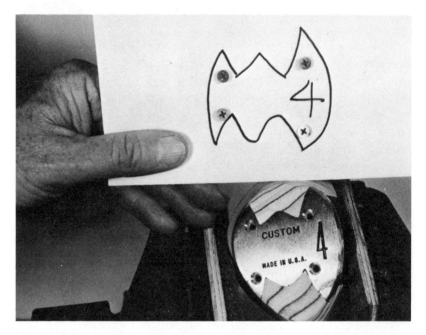

10-4. Using a suitably sized Phillips screwdriver, loosen the screws holding the sole plate in place. To be sure that each screw is returned to the same hole it came from, make a sole place design on a piece of heavy paper or light cardboard. Press each screw into its corresponding location on the paper. Be careful when handling the screws, for the edges are sometimes razor-sharp.

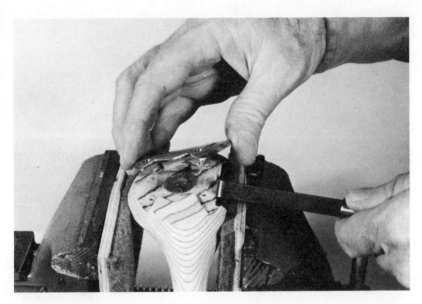

10-5. If you are lucky, the sole plate screws were tightened in the wood without epoxy. If they *do* resist removal, however, it is necessary to apply a spot of heat to each screw. Direct the flame of a small torch down the tube of a screw heater to focus the heat on the exact center of the screw head. Touch each screw head for a second or two with the flame, then let it set for 4 or 5 seconds. When the epoxy is softened, remove the screws. Once the screws are removed, run a thin steel blade or sole plate chisel between the metal of the sole plate and the wood of the insert and lift off the sole plate.

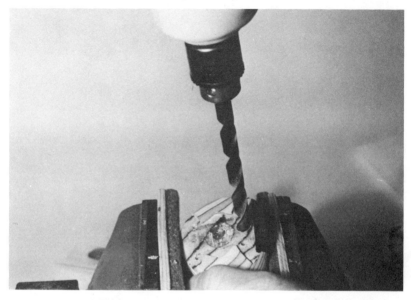

10-6. To add weight, drill a ⅜-inch hole just behind the insert (which is directly behind the center of impact on the hitting face).

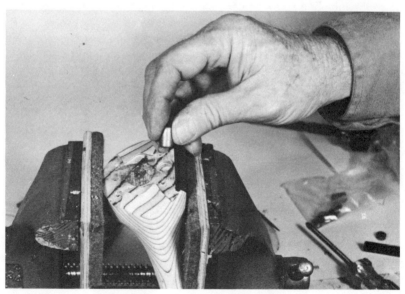

10-7. Drop in a standard-sized lead weight.

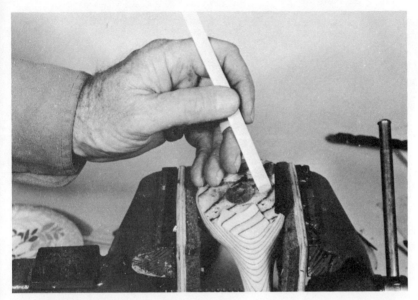

10-8. Then put a few drops of epoxy on top of the weight to secure it and prevent rattles.

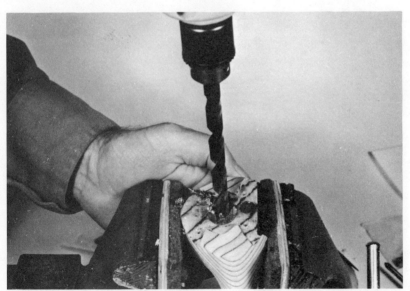

10-9. To reduce the weight of the club, use a ⅜-inch bit to drill out some of the lead weight that is under the center of the sole plate.

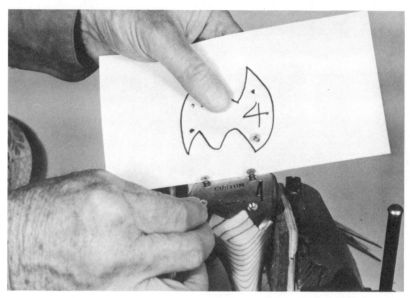

10-10. When you have the desired weight, replace the sole plate, returning each screw to its original hole.

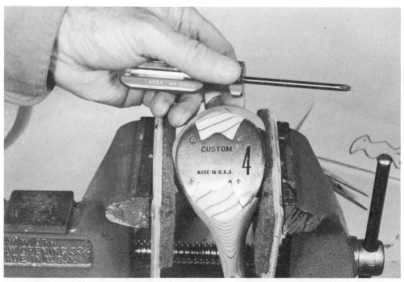

10-11. With the sole plate in place and its screws tightened, seal the areas where the sole plate and wood are joined with a bit of polyurethane finish applied with a small brush or cotton swab.

WOODS WITH METAL HEADS

Wood clubs with stainless steel heads are difficult to swing weight. They can be swing weighted with a little lead down the shaft or with lead tape opposite the hitting face. If you have aluminum alloy metal heads on your wood clubs, however, it is relatively easy to swing weight them by adding a swing weight adjustment port.

The process takes just a few minutes and requires a hand-held electric drill, a #21 drill, a small tap wrench, a #10-32 tap, #10-32 x ¼-inch allen screws, and a #3/32 allen wrench, a small metal punch, lead tape, and a swing weight scale.

To install a swing weight adjustment port, lock the club's head in a vise, using vise pads to protect wood and metal from the jaws of the vise. *Do not* apply too much pressure or you may pop out the wood inlay. With a metal punch, make a small mark in the alloy sole plate to keep the drill from skidding (Photo 10-12). With the hand-held drill, drill a hole through the sole plate (Photo 10-13). When the drill meets no more resis-

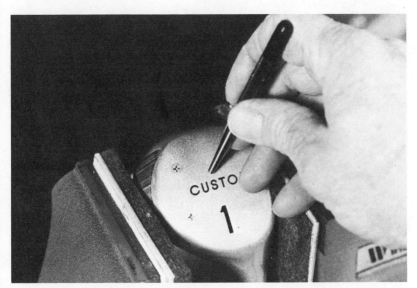

10-12. The first step to installing a swing weight adjustment port is locking the metal head in a vise and making a small mark in its plate with a metal punch.

tance, you have drilled through the alloy sole plate and into a small cavity between the metal and wood inlay. Lock the #10-32 tap into your tap wrench and carefully start the tap straight into the hole (Photo 10-14). Turn the wrench firmly to make new threads for the allen screw plug. Remove the tap and start one of the allen screws with the socket end out (Photo 10-15). If it fits, remove it; you are then ready to add lead weight. At this point, you may wish to install the shaft with epoxy, trim the butt end of the shaft, and install the grip.

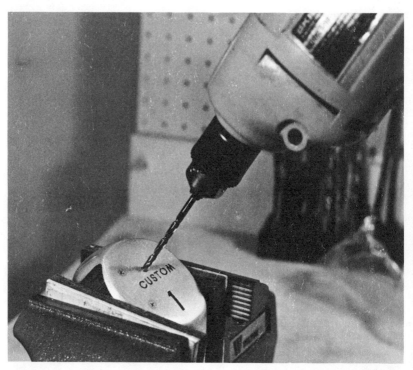

10-13. With a hand-held drill, drill a hole through the sole plate.

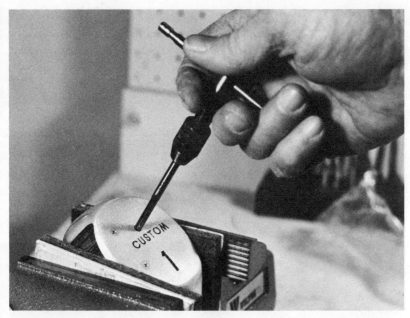

10-14. Start the tap straight into the hole, turning the tap wrench firmly to create new threads.

10-15. Start one of the allen screws into the hole to check for size.

To increase swing weight, you may add small lead shot, lead powder or filings, or 1-inch pieces of lead tape rolled lengthways into little rods, as in Photo 10-16. Lead tape is easy to use because two 1-inch sections of tape add about ½ point of swing weight. *Caution:* Add weight sparingly, for it is very difficult to remove.

To prevent a rattle, add absorbent cotton through the adjustment port. Screw in an allen screw. If it seems to fit loosely, add a drop or two of Lock-Tite. Do not screw too far or it will fall inside the cavity. Then spray the screw head with polyurethane spray to seal out moisture.

10-16. Adding rolled-up, 1-inch pieces of lead tape to the swing weight adjustment port is an easy way to increase the swing weight of a metal-headed wood.

10-17. The result: a professional-looking job of installing a swing weight adjustment port.

If you regularly work with golf clubs, your own or those of friends, you may well need a swing weight scale. It is beneficial for checking the swing weight of clubs after they undergo regripping, refinishing, reshafting, or any other repair that might change their swing weight.

11
CUSTOM BUILDING YOUR OWN CLUBS

There's always been a lot of mystery about how golf clubs are assembled, but there shouldn't be. Just keep in mind that, basically, a golf club head is glued onto a golf shaft with epoxy, the shaft is trimmed to length, and then a grip is put on. (Club head design and styling and swing weighting, while essential to the creation of a club, are not part of the club's assembly, which is the topic of this chapter.)

If you want a special head on a special shaft cut to a special length with a special grip, don't waste good golfing time running around to every golf shop in town, since they probably won't have just what you are looking for.

Instead, maybe you should assemble your own club. There's no reason why you can't build your own custom woods or irons, fancy putter, or special driver, for golf club assembly is really very simple. The parts can easily be ordered by mail, and you can easily assemble a full set of clubs in only a couple of evenings. By building your clubs yourself, you will save money and be sure of getting exactly the club you want.

This chapter discusses assembling wood clubs (including both woods with regular heads and woods with metal heads), assembling iron clubs (including both steel-shaft and graphite-shaft irons), and assembling a hickory-shaft putter and a goose-neck-mallet putter. The final section discusses how to do your own customizing of an unfinished deep-face driver.

ASSEMBLING WOODS

To assemble wood clubs you need to mail order a few basic materials: golf club heads, shafts, grips, and—for regular-headed woods only—rings, ferrules, backscrews, and whipping thread. Just remember that you must order a golf club shaft that has the same tip size that the club's head is bored for. For example, if the head is bored for a shaft with a .294 tip, then you must have a .294 tip shaft to go with it.

11-1. Parts and materials for assembling golf clubs: heads, shafts, golf shaft epoxy, and ferrules and rings for woods with wood heads.

Basic tools and materials you'll need to have on hand are golf shaft epoxy, a vise, a file, solvent, sandpaper, a shaft cutter, and an electric hand drill (all explained in Chapter 2).

REGULAR-HEADED WOODS

To assemble a wood club with a wood head, first slip the tip of the shaft into the wood head to see if it touches bottom. If it seems to bind just a little, pull the shaft out and check its tip for a bead or rim of chromium that sometimes forms there and keeps the shaft from fully seating. If there is such a bead, put the shaft in a vise and file it down carefully with a flat mill file. The shaft should then slip in.

Next position the rings and ferrule the correct distance up the shaft (Photo 11-2). Measure the distance that the shaft fits into the head and locate the ferrule so that it just touches the wood

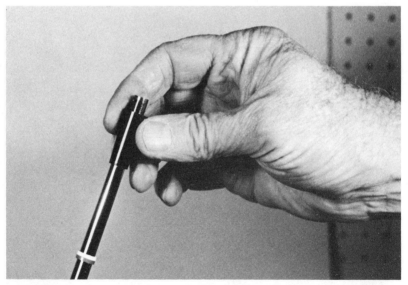

11-2. Fitting rings and a ferrule on the shaft of a wood.

when the shaft is fully seated. If the rings and ferrule are difficult to slip up the shaft, try slightly warming them by holding them about 8 inches over a low gas flame on the kitchen stove or heat them in a pan of warm water. When slightly heated, the rings and ferrule stretch just enough so that you can slide them up the shaft to where you want them.

The next step is to rough up the tip of the shaft with coarse sandpaper. This gives the epoxy a rough surface to grab onto, and you get a better bond. Then mix equal portions of parts A and B of the golf shaft epoxy in a disposable container with a wooden stirrer. Coat the tip of the shaft generously with epoxy and slip it into the hosel of the wood (Photo 11-3). Twirl the head around a few times to distribute the epoxy evenly, remove the shaft to add more epoxy to its tip, and reinsert it. Use plenty of epoxy, and wipe off the excess.

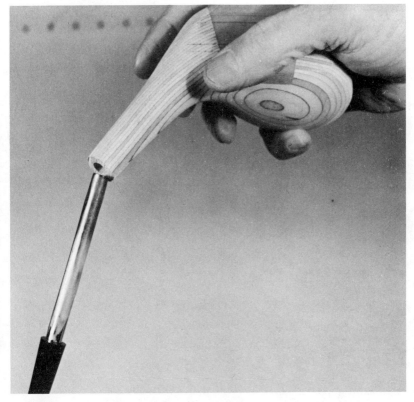

11-3. Test the shaft in the club head first. Then coat the tip of the shaft liberally with epoxy and slip the shaft into the head.

With a driving plug in the open butt of the shaft, tape the plug firmly a few times to seat the shaft. Then stand the club up to dry overnight. Stand it exactly vertical so that the epoxy will remain well-distributed around the shaft. Place it in a warm place, such as near a furnace, for epoxy bonds better and faster when the temperature is around 75°F. The next day, test the bond by trying to twist the shaft.

If you're really going to do a professional job, the wood head must be pinned to the shaft with what is called a steel *backscrew* or *lockscrew*. With a 7/16-inch drill bit in your electric hand drill, drill right through the back of the hosel about ¾ inch above the heel of the club. Drill through the shaft and all, about 1¹⁄₁₆ inch into the wood. Then drive a steel backscrew firmly into place.

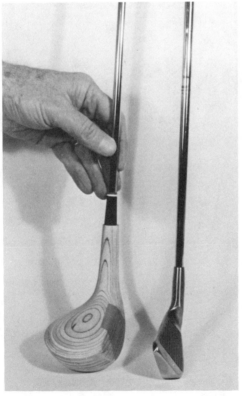

11-4. To set the epoxy correctly, stand both woods and irons in an exact vertical position so that the epoxy is well-distributed.

Notice the small step where the wood meets the plastic ferrule. Sand this bump with a sanding drum on an electric drill or strips of sandpaper so that the wood is flush with the ferrule to provide a smooth surface for the whipping.

Finish the head according to Chapter 5, wrap the whipping thread according to Chapter 6, trim the shaft, and install a grip of your choice according to Chapter 4. The result will be a brand-new, custom-built wood club with a wood head.

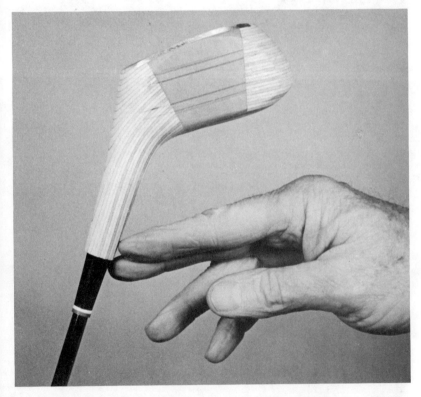

11-5. When the epoxy has set, the wood must be sanded flush with the ferrule.

METAL-HEADED WOODS

Wood clubs with metal heads are even easier to assemble than those with regular heads. Metal-headed clubs require no rings and ferrules, no pinning the head and shaft together with a backscrew, no wrapping with whipping thread, and, of course, no finishing of the head.

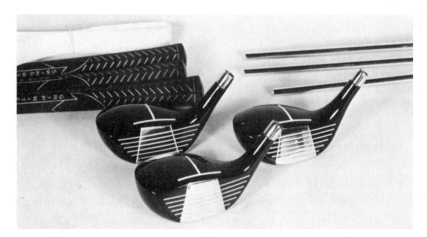

11-6. With these materials, you can assemble a fine set of metal headed woods: a driver head, a 3 wood head, and a 4 wood head; three Green Victory grips; three strips of golf shaft tape; and three True Temper shafts with reinforced tips. These shafts were made especially for metal-headed woods because their shaft cavities are only about 1½ inches deep (instead of the 4 inches of a wood head's cavity) and therefore take more strain at the tip of the shaft.

11-7. Golf shaft epoxy, a shaft cutter, and a file or two are necessary for assembling metal-headed wood clubs.

The first step in assembling these clubs involves testing the tip of each shaft by placing it in one of the heads (Photo 11-8). If the shaft does not seat all the way, check its tip for a bead or rim of chromium that sometimes forms there. If such a bead is present, put the shaft in a vise and file the bead off completely (Photo 11-9).

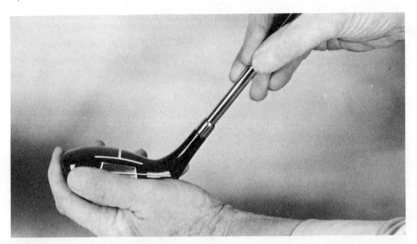

11-8. Test each shaft in a metal head to ensure that the tip does not bind and can be fully seated.

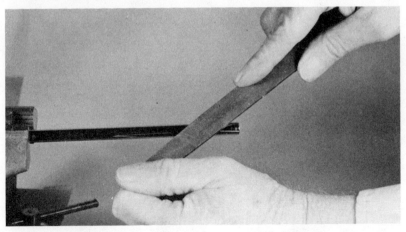

11-9. If the shaft seems a bit too tight, file down its tip until it slips into the head easily.

Once sure that the shaft tips are the correct size, rough up each tip with coarse sandpaper so that the epoxy has a rough surface on which to bond. Then use a round file to remove any extra-sharp edges on the inside edge of each head's hosel.

Mix the epoxy and liberally coat the tip of a shaft, slip it into the head, twirl it around, remove the tip, add more epoxy to it, and then reinsert it into the shaft. Wipe off any excess epoxy. Let the club stand overnight. Once the epoxy is set, trim the butt end of each shaft to the desired length. Then wrap the shaft with tape and install the grips of your choice. (See Chapter 4 for instructions on grip installation.)

The result is a custom-built wood club with just the type of shaft, length, and grip that you want.

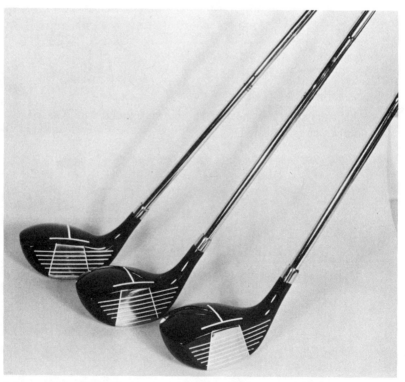

11-10. Once the epoxy has set, trim the shaft and install your choice of grip. You then have a fine set of metal-headed woods.

ASSEMBLING IRONS

To assemble iron clubs, you must order the basic materials—heads, shafts, and grips. Most iron heads are bored for .355 shafts, so be sure to order iron shafts with .355 tips. The usual basic tools discussed in Chapter 3 should be on hand.

Assembling either steel-shaft or graphite-shaft irons is very similar to assembling metal-headed woods. Irons, like metal-headed woods, require no backscrew, no whipping thread, and no finishing. They may or may not require a ferrule and rings.

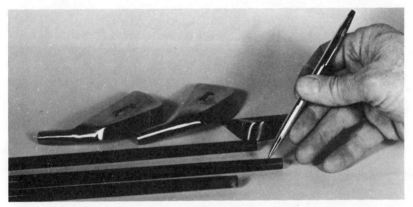

11-11. Irons may have steel or graphite shafts. These are graphite shafts.

Before beginning assembly, slip each shaft into the hosel of the iron head to be sure of a good fit—tight but not binding. If a *steel* shaft is too tight, file off any bead or rim of chromium plating that may have formed at the tip of the shaft. If a *graphite* shaft is a bit too tight, sand a little graphite off to bring the shaft's diameter down a couple of thousandths of an inch so that it will fit into the iron head's neck. The makers of graphite shafts suggest that, with the head in a vise and a round file in hand, you round off the sharp inside corner at the top of the neck. This procedure, as shown in Photo 11-12, prevents the sharp corners from cutting into the graphite fibers every time the ball is hit. Such a procedure is not necessary with steel-shaft irons.

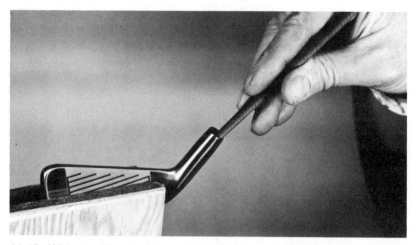

11-12. With graphite-shaft irons, it is advisable to file off the sharp inside corner of the shaft cavity of the head to minimize strain to the tip of the shaft.

Next, mix some golf shaft epoxy and apply it liberally to the tip of the shaft. Slip the shaft down inside the neck of the iron, twirl it around a few times, remove the tip, apply a little more epoxy, reinsert the tip, and stand the club up in a warm place to dry overnight.

11-13. Coat the tip of the shaft liberally with golf shaft epoxy, slip it into the head, and twirl it around.

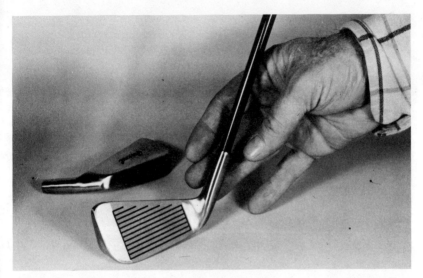

11-14. Stand the iron club up to dry overnight.

The next day, trim each shaft to the desired length. If the club has a steel shaft, use a shaft cutter, as described in Chapter 9. But do *not* use a shaft cutter for a graphite shaft. Instead, wrap the point at which you wish to cut the shaft with a couple of tight turns of masking tape. Then, on the masking tape, mark the exact spot where the shaft is to be cut. (See Photo 11-15). Then, with a hacksaw, cut through the tape and all.

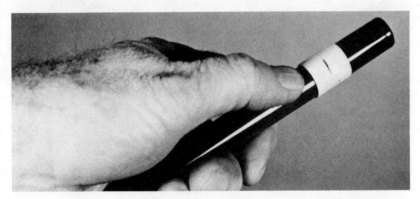

11-15. The thumb is pointing to the butt end of a graphite shaft. Once the shafts are installed, trim each graphite shaft with a hacksaw.

When all the shafts are trimmed, install the grips of your choice, as described in Chapter 4.

ASSEMBLING PUTTERS

This section discusses how to assemble two favorite kinds of putters, a hickory-shaft putter and a gooseneck-mallet putter. Building either of these fine clubs is simple, can be done in a couple of evenings with mail-ordered parts, and costs much less than buying the clubs ready-made.

HICKORY-SHAFT PUTTER

It is often difficult to find a hickory-shaft putter with a head design you want. So why not custom build one yourself? The parts that you must order are a putter head, a shaft, a couple of strips of golf grip tape, and a leather strip with end cap (for creating an old-fashioned 18-inch grip).

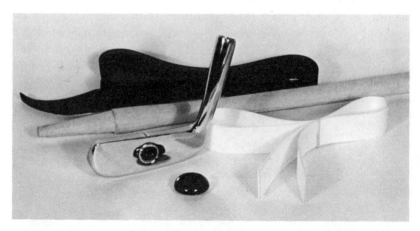

11-16. Building a hickory-shaft putter requires a putter head, a hickory shaft, two strips of tape, a long strip of leather, and a plastic end cap.

Hickory shafts come with an oversized tip, but the shaft must fit into a metal putter head with a hosel bored for a regular .355 tip. To fit the hickory shaft into the head's neck, first measure the depth of the shaft cavity and mark it off on the tip with a lead pencil. Cut off the tip at that point with a hacksaw or wood saw. Then file down the tip of the shaft with a wood file (Photo 11-17) until the tip is .355 inch in diameter. Check the fit of the shaft tip in the cavity frequently while filing.

The next step is cementing the tip of the shaft into the club's head with plenty of epoxy (Photo 11-18). Stand it up to set overnight. The next day, carefully file the hickory flush where it meets the metal.

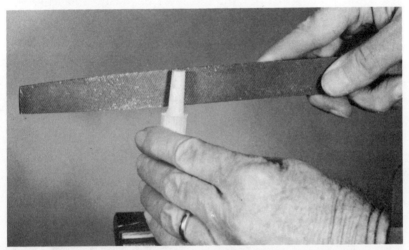

11-17. With a coarse file, remove wood from the tip of the hickory shaft until it fits into the hosel of the putter.

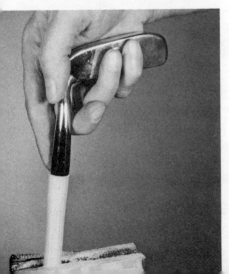

11-18. Cement the shaft into place with epoxy and let it stand overnight to dry.

Trim the shaft with a hacksaw or wood saw to the length you desire. (A shaft cutter will not do because hickory is so extra-hard.) With a ¼-inch drill bit, drill a hole for the center screw to go through the black plastic end cap and into the wood at the butt end of the shaft. It will be necessary to file or sand the cap down until it is the same diameter that the butt end of the grip will be. Use a flat mill file or small sanding disk on your electric drill to file it down to size. Smooth out any roughness by wiping the end cap with a little acetone on a cotton swab. The acetone will immediately dissolve the top layer of plastic and leave the end cap with a high-gloss finish.

11-19. Trim the hickory shaft to the desired length and fasten the filed-down end cap to the butt end of the shaft.

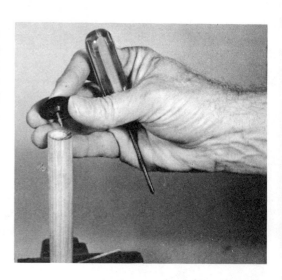

·Next, to prepare the hickory shaft for the wrap-on leather grip, first wrap the golf grip tape around the shaft just under the end cap. Starting from the circular band of tape at the butt end of the shaft, spiral wrap the rest of the tape down the shaft in a clockwise direction, leaving about 1/8 inch between turns. Leave the outer piece of release paper on the tape at this stage. When you come to the end of a strip of tape, start the next strip and continue spiral wrapping down the shaft for 18 to 20 inches.

Begin wrapping the leather strip with the end of the strip that has an angle cut, as shown in Photo 11-20. Place the edge of the

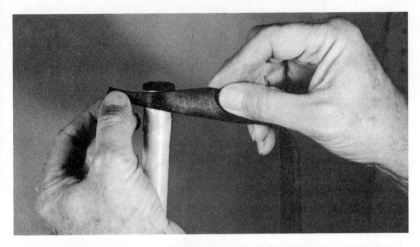

11-20. Once the shaft is covered with a layer of double-face tape, start the leather strip, angle-cut end first, just under the end cap.

angle flat against the overhang of the end cap. Bring the leather around counterclockwise and overlap the tip of the leather strip for about 1 or 1½ inches. Then spiral wrap the leather strip down the hickory shaft, holding the shaft firmly in your right hand and pulling the leather strip with your left, and overlapping or butting each turn of the strip by about 1/16 to 1/8 inch. (See Photo 11-21).

11-21. Overlap the leather slightly as you spiral wrap down the shaft.

At the bottom of the grip, cut the leather straight across with a single-edge razor blade. Wrap a piece of black vinyl electrician's tape a couple of turns around the bottom to secure the leather.

Finish the hickory shaft with wipe-on stain and spray the shaft with polyurethane finish, as described in Chapter 5. The result will be a beautiful hickory-shaft putter ready to take to the putting green.

11-22. Trim the leather square at the bottom of the grip and wrap the raw edges of leather with black electrician's tape to complete the grip.

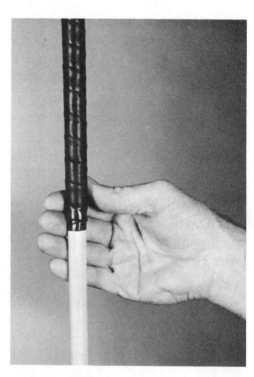

Assembling a Gooseneck Mallet Putter

This gooseneck mallet putter (Photo 11-23) is a new, up-to-date version of the famous wooden mallet putter that every golfer knows. The big difference in this goosenecck putter is in design. There is a bend or twist in the gooseneck of the putter, an offset so that a golfer sighting down the shaft sees the center of the ball rather than the leading edge of the hitting face.

11-23. The gooseneck putter is a beautiful and accurate club that's easy to build.

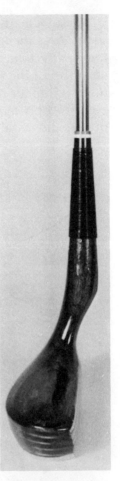

11-24. Parts of a gooseneck putter.

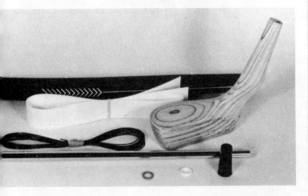

Building one of these gooseneck putters is really very simple whether you buy all the parts separately or get a complete kit. In just a couple of evenings, even the novice golf club assembler can put together a completely finished gooseneck putter that's a beauty. The parts necessary to assemble a gooseneck putter are shown in Photo 11-24: a steel shaft with a .294 tip; an unfinished laminated maple head, already shaped and sanded, that has a heavy metal sole plate and scoring on its hitting face; golf grip tape and a rubber or leather slip-on grip; a ferrule and two rings; and a hank of whipping thread.

To assemble the putter, first fit the rings and ferrule onto the shaft. Press them just far enough up the shaft so that the shaft touches the bottom of the shaft cavity of the neck. Rough up the metal tip of the shaft with sandpaper, coat the tip with epoxy, insert it into the neck, and twirl it around to distribute the epoxy evenly. Apply more epoxy, seat the shaft fully in the neck of the putter, and stand it upright for the epoxy to set overnight.

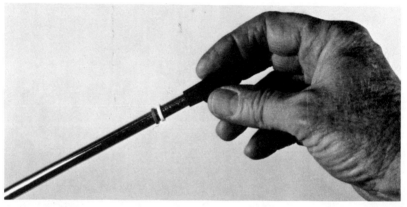

11-25. First fit the rings and ferrule onto the shaft.

11-26. Then spread epoxy on the tip.

The next day, examine the point where the wood and ferrule come together (Photo 11-27). With the shaft in a vise, go around the ferrule with a strip of sandpaper until the ferrule is absolutely flush with the wood (Photo 11-28). This provides a smooth base for the whipping thread.

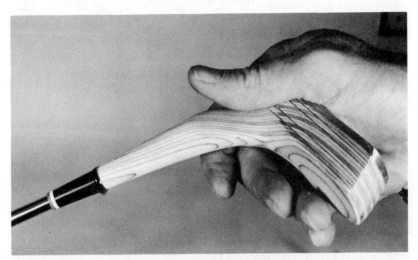

11-27. Examine your work to make sure the epoxy has dried.

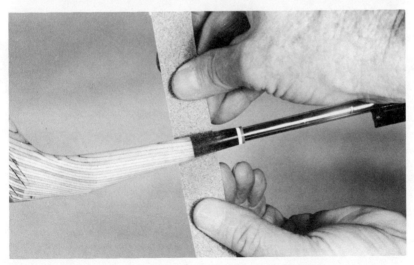

11-28. Sand the ferrule flush with the wood for a smooth surface.

To finish the gooseneck putter, follow the procedure for refinishing woods described in Chapter 5 (Photos 11-29 through 11-31). Once the head has been stained, the polyurethane finish can be applied either by spraying as described in Chapter 5 or by dipping. For a *dip* finish, dip the entire head in a dipping can of polyurethane finish (Photo 11-32). Hold the putter over the can for a minute to let the excess run off. Then hold the putter with its head upright and twirl it between your fingers while checking for runs or sags. Remove a run before it sets by wiping it downward with a tip of the finger. Stand the club upright to dry overnight.

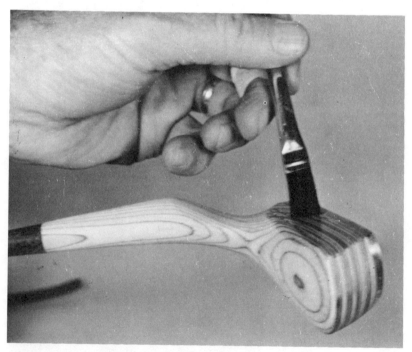

11-29. Before staining, brush sealer on the hitting face.

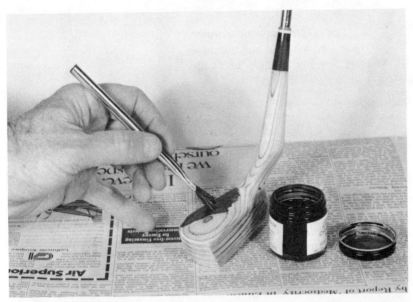

11-30. Cover the head with stain completely—except for the hitting face.

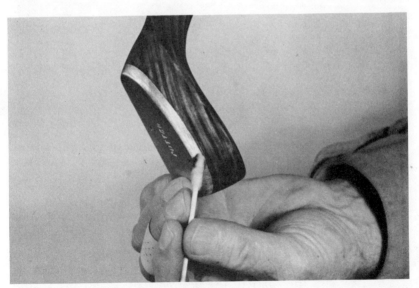

11-31. To remove any extra stain that got onto the sole plate use a cotton swab dipped in rubbing alcohol.

11-32. Dipping the gooseneck putter head into a can of polyurethane finish is one way to apply the finish.

The next day, examine the head for dust specks and blemishes. It's a good idea to rub it down lightly with extra-fine steel wool. Then give the club a second dipping, following the same procedure as before.

After another night of drying, wind the whipping thread, starting just below the rings and ending about 1½ inches below the ferrule. Follow the whipping procedure described in Chapter 6.

Finally, trim the shaft to the desired length and install the putter grip, using extra layers of tape if necessary. Gripping is described in Chapter 4.

Let the polyurethane finish cure for about three or four days, and then drop the putter into your golf bag. If you like the sensitive touch of a wood putter and an offset head, chances are this gooseneck putter will become your favorite.

CUSTOMIZING A DEEP-FACE DRIVER

If you've ever watched the big hitter in a long driving contest crunch the ball halfway into the next county, you can bet the golf shirt on your back, he's hitting with a deep-face driver.

A *deep-face driver* is a special kind of driver with an extra-big wood head and an extra-big hitting face. The extra hitting area means you can get more solid wood on the ball and hit more straight, long shots. With a deep-face driver, a golfer should have fewer topped balls dribbling off the tee and should sky fewer balls that resemble infield pop-ups at the baseball park. With this club, once your club head speed is up into the 105 to 107 mph range, you will start getting those dream hits.

Your pro shop probably does not carry this special kind of club, but by customizing an unfinished driver, you get exactly what you want for a lot less money.

The mail-ordered deep-face driver in Photo 11-33 comes fine-sanded and ready for finishing, with a regular-flex or stiff-flex

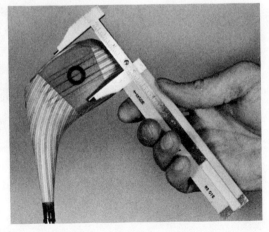

11-33. The deep-face driver, which has 40 percent more hitting area than a regular driver, comes unfinished as shown here. The club's shaft, insert, and sole plate come already installed.

shaft already mounted and pinned in the head and with the insert and sole plates mounted in place. In short, the club is ready for you to customize and finish yourself.

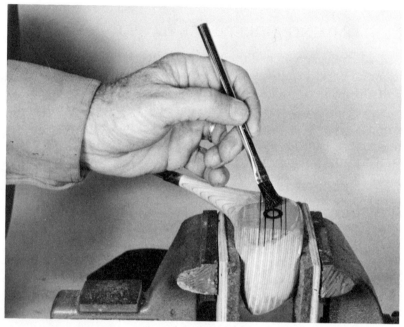

11-34. To finish the deep-face driver, seal the hitting face with sealer that comes in a refinishing kit. Sealer prevents stray drops of stain from penetrating the face.

You can alter the hitting face any way you want. You can give it a slice face to correct a hook or give it a slight hook to correct your slice. Also you can give the club more or less loft on the hitting face.

Then you can stain the deep-face driver any color you want, dip or spray the polyurethane finish, cut the 44-inch shaft to whatever length you desire, and choose from about 60 styles and colors of golf grips. That's really customizing a club!

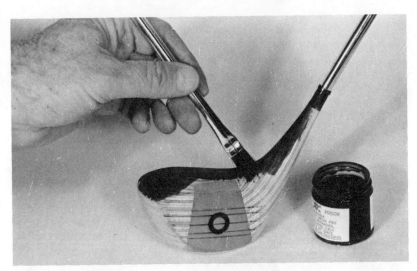

11-35. Brush stain on the wood surfaces. Choose from black, cherry red, mahogany, walnut, and armour red stain.

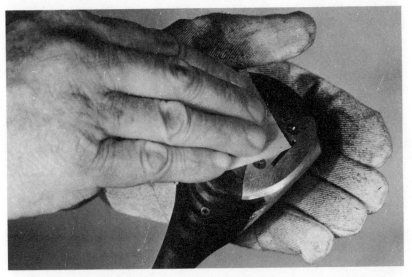

11-36. When the stain is dry, rub the head lightly with gritty sandpaper or fine steel wool to knock off any dust particles or specks.

11-37. Clean off any wood stain on the metal sole plate with a cotton swab dipped in rubbing alcohol.

11-38. To apply the polyurethane finish, either use the dip method or use a spray can.

GLOSSARY

ADDRESS: The position of a golfer when he is ready to start his backswing.

ARTHRITIC GRIP: A specially shaped or large-size grip for players with stiff or arthritic fingers and hands. Provides a better grip than regular size grips.

BACKWEIGHT: A contoured brass weight fastened with screws to the back of a wood head opposite the hitting face. Claimed to get the ball up faster. Backweight may also be lead plug inserted in the butt end of the golf shaft to lessen swing weight and improve control.

BUFFING COMPOUND: A very fine-grained, gritty material used to polish iron heads. It may be as fine as 600 or 800 grit.

BULGE: The slight convex curve on the hitting face of a wood, measured from side to side. Roll is a convex curve measured from top to bottom.

BUTT: The large end of a golf shaft where the grip is installed.

BUTT DIAMETER: Diameter of the large or butt end of a golf shaft measured in thousandths of an inch as .580″ or .600″ butt diameter. Important in fitting grips.

COLLAR: A black plastic trim to give a neater appearance to the lower end of a golf grip. Necessary for leather grips which have raw edges at the bottom. Also called the "Grip Collar."

DECAL: A water or solvent transfer design applied to the top of finished wood head to denote the club maker's name or the brand name.

DRIVER: The 1 wood used for hitting tee shots at the beginning of play on each hole.

EXTENDERS OR SHAFT EXTENDERS: Section of steel tubing epoxied into butt end of shaft to lengthen clubs. A new grip is then installed over the extender.

FACE: Also called Hitting Face. The front hitting surface of an iron or wood head. The face makes contact with the ball.

FACE ANGLE: Any variation of the hitting face from 90° to the intended line of flight. With a square face at a right angle, the face angle is 0°. With a slice or open face, the angle might be 1° or 2° slice. With a closed or hook face, the angle might be 1° or 2° hook.

FERRULES OR FERRULES AND RINGS: Plastic trim mounted on the shaft just above the hosel of woods and irons.

FILLER: A finishing material used to fill in the pores of a wood head. Usually applied after the stain and before the clear finish coats. Necessary in refinishing persimmon heads.

FLEX: Measurement of the degree of stiffness in a golf shaft. It ranges from Ladies, A Flex, and Regular to Stiff and Extra-Stiff.

GRIP: The rubber or leather part which fits over the butt end of the shaft and by which the club is held.

HEAD: The steel or wooden piece designed to strike the ball.

HEAD SPEED: A measurement of the head velocity at the point of the swing where the club head strikes the ball. The faster the head speed, the more distance you get. Normal range is from 80 mph to 107 or 108 mph.

HEEL: The angle at which the sole of the head turns upward to the neck or hosel of the club.

HOOKFACE: A wood club with a face angle that gives the ball a counterclockwise spin producing a hook. Used to overcome a tendency to slice.

HOSEL: The "neck" of an iron or wood head.

INSERT SCREWS: Brass screws used to secure the insert in a wood club.

INSERTS: The plastic, epoxy, or metal piece in the center of the hitting face of a wood to take the impact of hitting the ball.

IRONS: Clubs with a stainless steel or a chrome-plated forging head. For fairway play. Normally 10 to a set: 2-9, PW, SW.

KINETIC GRIP: A grip with an extra-large core size to fit Kinetic shafts with .665 to .710 diameter butt sizes.

LAMINATED HEAD: Wood head made of many thin layers of wood with the grain going in alternate directions at right angles for strength. Usually applies to laminated maple heads.

LEAD WEIGHT: The lead plug under the sole plate of a wood head.

LEATHER GRIP: A spiral leather wrapping on a molded rubber core.

LIE: Measurement of the angle between the shaft and horizontal when the sole of the head is grounded in the address position.

LOCKSCREW SCREWS: Steel backscrews or pins. Used to secure a wood head on a steel shaft.

LOFT: Angle of the hitting face from the perpendicular. A driver with a loft of 11° has a hitting face that is angled back 11° from perpendicular at the top of the face.

OFFSET: A style of clubhead design where the shaft is in advance of the hitting face. More common in putter heads.

OVER-THE-HOSEL: A style of iron and putter construction where the steel shaft fits over the hosel rather than inside the hosel.

PAINT FILL: Colored paint used in the grooves of a wood face for a decorative effect. May also be the colored paint in stampings on a sole plate or an iron head.

PARALLEL TIP: The small or tip end of a golf shaft made cylindrical, without taper.

PERSIMMON WOOD: A tough, close-grained native American wood greatly prized as material for deluxe wood heads. Very beautiful grain and appearance when finished.

RATTLE: Noise emanating from a loose head or loose shaft or from a loose weight inside the shaft.

REAMER: A tapered drilling or boring tool used to bore out wooden or iron heads for the desired size shaft.

REFINISHING KIT: A blister-packed kit containing golf wood finish remover, sealer, stain, and spray finish with enough material to refinish one or two sets of woods.

REINFORCED TIP SHAFT: A specially made shaft with thicker walls at the tip for use in the new metal head woods.

RESHAFTING: Removing and replacing a broken shaft in a wood or iron. Can mean removing shafts of one flex and replacing with shafts of a different flex or different length.

ROLL: Convex curve of the hitting face of a wood from top to bottom. Believed to help put desired spin on ball.

SANDBLASTED AREA: The rough area on the hitting face of an iron that puts backspin on the ball.

SLICE FACE: Wood head so constructed that it gives the ball a clockwise spin, causing it to curve off to the right of the line of flight. An open face.

SOLE: The flat bottom section of a wood or iron club. The part that rests on the ground.

SOLE PLATE: The brass or white metal plate designed to protect the surface on the bottom of wood heads from wear during play.

SOLEPLATE SCREWS: Stubby brass screws used to secure a sole plate in the mortise on a wood head.

SQUARE FACE: Wood head constructed so that the hitting face is at right angles with a line of flight to the target. A wood face with zero degrees slice or hook.

STAINS: Colored pigment in a liquid carrier to give wood heads a rich, luxurious color.

STARTER: A small, tapered plastic tool used to press grip collars over the open butt end of a steel shaft before slip-on grips are installed.

SWINGWEIGHT: A method of constructing and weighting clubs so that each club, long or short shaft, has the same smooth feel or swingweight when hitting.

SWINGWEIGHT SCALE: A balance device used to measure the swingweight of clubs so that weight can be added or taken away to give each club the same swingweight.

TAPE: Special two-sided tape with adhesive on both sides. Used in mounting slip-on rubber and leather grips.

TAPER TIP: The small or tip end of a golf shaft designed with a taper to fit into a wood or iron head.

TORQUE: The twisting force on a shaft when a club is swung. Too much torque means the hitting face is not square at the moment of impact.

UNDERLISTING: The floppy rubber sleeve with an end cap which forms the base for a leather wrap-on grip.

VISE CLAMP: A rubber block split halfway through that is used to protect a golf shaft from the jaws of a vise in making club repairs.

WHIPPING OR WRAPPING: The nylon winding thread that is tightly wrapped around the neck of a wood club to protect the wood from splitting.

WHIPPING COVER: A tapered black sleeve of heat-shrink plastic used on the hosel of a wood instead of whipping.

WRAP-ON GRIP: A special grip consisting of a separate rubber core (underlisting) and a leather strip which is wrapped on by hand.

INDEX